A View from the Porch

Ludlow Porch

A View from the Porch

Peachtree Publishers Limited

Published by
PEACHTREE PUBLISHERS, LTD.
494 Armour Circle, N. E.
Atlanta, Georgia 30324

Manufactured in the United States of America

Text and Cover Design by Joan Stoliar

4th printing

ISBN: 0-931948-17-7
Library of Congress Catalog Card Number 81-80383

Dedication

I thank God that I have been allowed to know many independent ladies in my life. This book is therefore respectfully dedicated to:

My Grandmother Kidd, who taught me to pray and expect an answer.

My Aunt Evelyn, who taught me never to butter a whole piece of bread, and that manners are important no matter where you are. For that I owe her more than I can ever repay.

To my Aunt Kat, who taught me that reading is a very important adventure, and who read me *Gone With the Wind*, cover to cover, before I was six years old. Oh! how I love that redheaded lady.

To Diane, who laughs at my jokes, holds my hand, and loves me when I need it most.

To Barbara and Leigh Ann. All gifts from God are special. Barbara and Leigh Ann are extra special.

To my Nanny, who went to join my father on February 9, 1977. She was my mother and my best friend. I miss her more every time the clock ticks.

Contents

Unforgettable—and Forgettable—Characters

Trivia

Life on the Radio

About once a week, someone asks me, "How did you get into radio?"

I have heard a couple of versions and, while they make good conversation, they are not accurate. Here is how it all started:

Several years ago I was on a deer hunt in Demopolis, Alabama. I was having a delightful dinner at Louise's when the waitress came up and said I had a phone call. There was no way to know it then, but that phone call was about to change my life.

It was from my stepbrother, Lewis Grizzard. In addition to being the executive sports editor of *The Atlanta Journal,* Lewis also did some work for *Sports Illustrated* magazine. *Sports Illustrated* had sent telegrams to their people all over the country, saying they were going to do a story on trivia and were trying to find the best trivia players in the country.

The telegram had said they wanted to find colorful characters like old guys who answered trivia questions in bars for free drinks.

Well, Lewis sent them my name and explained that, while he didn't know any trivia players like they described, he did know a burly ex-Marine intellectual who was a good trivia player.

I told him that it sounded like it might be fun, and

we talked for a while about other things. After we hung up, I promptly forgot about *Sports Illustrated*.

I guess about a month went by, and one day I got a call from San Francisco. The caller identified himself as Ron Fimrite and said he was doing a story on trivia players for *Sports Illustrated*. He said he wanted to fly to Atlanta and play some trivia with me. We chatted briefly, and a couple of days later he showed up in my office to interview me.

He had said on the phone that it would take about an hour. Well, he was one of the nicest guys I had ever talked to. We chatted in my office for a couple of hours, then went out and played trivia all through a three-hour lunch. I put him on an airplane that night and thought to myself how much fun it would be to see my name in *Sports Illustrated*.

The magazine held up the story for a couple of months, but it finally came out in March. I got calls from old friends I hadn't heard from in years. I got several middle-of-the-night calls from drunks— some I knew and some I didn't.

Then one day I got a call from a lady at WRNG radio. She said one of the talk show hosts, Bob Mohan, would like me to be a guest on his Sunday show. I was a big Bob Mohan fan, and thought: "This sounds like fun; I can play a little trivia and meet a man I really admire at the same time."

In those days WRNG carried stock car races on the weekend. Bob's show came on right after the races.

It's real tough to get calls after a long day of racing. I have always felt that there was a simple explanation for that—everybody turns his radio off when the races start.

Bob met me at the door, and since no one had ever played trivia on the radio, he was justifiably worried about how it would go, especially after a race. He said, "I tell you what. We'll try this for about twenty or thirty minutes to see how it goes."

In our first thirty minutes on the air, we received over 2,500 calls. Mohan and I hit it off in the first five minutes, and our Sunday afternoon get-together started a friendship that continues to this day.

I got to tell you, funseekers, I was hooked from the minute that microphone light came on.

It's very difficult to explain, but deep down I knew that broadcasters had to be the happiest people on earth and some way, somehow, I had to find a way to do it again.

The next phone call I got was from WSB radio, a fine station that I had grown up with. They wanted me to be a guest on "The Voice of the South." I went down and did an hour special and once again had the time of my life.

I really had the bug now, and radio had become my hobby. Another call from WRNG, another show, then another and another.

I was still working hard as an insurance claims adjuster. My business was growing; I had offices in Atlanta, Macon, and Athens, but deep down in my mind I was thinking that if I could make a living in radio, it would be like retiring.

Ben Baldwin had been in Atlanta radio for a number of years, and at this point was the acting program director at WRNG. He called me one day and said that he had heard me as a guest on Bob Mohan's show, and later as a caller to Mohan. He said he liked my sense of humor, and he would like for me to come out and do one hour a day for a week. I think somebody was out sick or on vacation, and the only thing he could promise was one week, one hour a day. I was to be paid the princely sum of $10 for this effort.

I explained to Ben that I had a business to run, and didn't know if I could spare the time. Even while I was protesting, I was thinking: "Oh, Lord, let him talk me into it!"

Well, he did talk me into it. I went to WRNG for one week, and I'm still there, thanks in great part to Ben.

The first week I was there, I did my first spoof about a sissy prize fighter named Ralph Raindrop. If I do say so myself, it was funny as hell, and the audience ate it up. There were over fifty calls at the front desk about how funny it was. Management, however, was not as thrilled about it as the audience was. Ben Baldwin was called in and asked what that maniac, Porch, was doing. Ben went to bat for me and finally wound up in a screaming match with the general manager.

After his bout with management, Ben came to me and said, "What you did today was funny. Don't let anybody change what you do."

Ben helped me polish my style, and for the rest of the time he was at WRNG he offered me help and encouragement.

I owe a lot to Ben, more than I can repay.

Whenever I'm asked by a youngster how to get into the radio broadcasting business, I always say, "Go to school, learn the business, and then be in the right place at the right time."

My years in radio have been very satisfying, and I never made a dime that I didn't feel like I had stolen.

If they ever find out that I would do it free, I'm in Big Trouble.

A Wrestler's Mama Is Important

I had been waiting a long time for this; my first assignment as a sports reporter. WRNG had promised me for almost six years that they would give me a chance to be a big-time sports reporter, and finally the big night was here.

As I was driving into the parking lot at the city auditorium, I couldn't help but think, "Luddy, you've come a long way from Snellville, being allowed to cover the wrestling matches for a big-time radio station."

I finally found a parking place between two pickup trucks and made my way to the ticket line. The man in line behind me was wearing an STP T-shirt. He smiled at me and said, "This is your first time at the matches, ain't it?"

I said, "Sure is. How could you tell?"

He giggled and said, "You're wearin' a tie. I can spot a greenhorn ever time."

I apologized for being overdressed, got my ticket, and made my way to the balcony. The first match was already under way when I got to my seat. The fat lady behind me was screaming. I couldn't get all she said, but she was saying some bad things about the mama of one of the wrestlers.

The first seventeen or eighteen matches were uneventful. As a matter of fact, the most exciting thing that happened during those matches was when the fat lady threw up on the policeman who was leading her away.

Intermission time came, and everybody was anxious for the main event to start. You could feel the electricity in the air. Then suddenly I saw him, standing there on the stage in all his slick headed, evil ugliness—the hated Abdullah the Butcher.

The crowd went crazy, and there was a lot more screaming about his mama. It seems wrestling fans put a lot of stock into who your mama is.

Abdullah made his way to the ring, where his opponent was waiting. He was going to wrestle with a right nice old boy named Dory Funk, Jr. You know he was a nice fellow, because he was wearing a football jacket and a white cowboy hat. I'm not sure what happened next, but it looked like while they were being introduced, Abdullah grabbed the microphone out of Freddy Miller's hand and hit Dory right on the head. They disqualified Abdullah for not being a nice person and for carrying a knife.

I had a lot better time than Dory, and who knows? This week the wrestling matches, next week the Super Bowl.

Awful Knawful Rides Again

It's that time of year again, and I just know you know what I mean. I guess everybody has his special time of the year. To some folks it's Christmas with the presents, decorations, and jolly old St. Nick. Other folks just can't wait for the football season to start, and the outdoor people just can't wait for the hunting season to start. And who doesn't love the springtime, especially in Atlanta with the dogwoods, jonquils, and Andy Griffith reruns?

Yes, sir. Every time of the year is special to somebody, and this is my favorite time, because as the program chairman for the Snellville Knights of Pythias, I get to announce on the radio that plans for this year's poke sallet festival are under way. It looks like this festival may be the biggest in our history.

All the regular events that you have grown to love over the years will still be happening. But this year we have added some very interesting events. For example, this year we are having an Atlanta Braves pitch, hit, and error contest, a real fun event, and it's open to any awkward child under twelve.

And the Jack Lescoulie Look-Alike contest is sure to be a crowd-pleaser.

Speaking of crowd-pleasers, at the half-time entertainment of the tire-changing contest we're going to present, by popular demand, our local daredevil, Awful Knawful, jumping a 1958 Cadillac over twelve motorcycles.

And musical entertainment! Let me tell you about the musical entertainment! The one and only Wilson Babcock will be there with his *entire* collection of 78 rpm records! Can you stand it?

Funseekers, make your plans now to be there, because the first fifteen people to show up at Mama Leoni's will get a free slice of collard pizza. And for you TV fans, a very, very special announcement: Officer Don will not be in the parade this year.

I promise you, this year's poke sallet festival is going to make the Mardi Gras look like a quiet Sunday in Rockmart.

When you do a radio talk show, one of the fringe benefits is the interesting and famous people you get to meet.

You get call after call from folks who want to be on the air. You hear from public relations people, you hear from publishing companies who want to have their newest author on. You hear from movie studios who want to plug their latest pictures.

Politicians always like to talk to the voters, and then there are folks who have new products on the market, and they want to promote sales by drumming up excitement on the radio.

You also get a lot of calls from folks with an ax to grind. I mean, people who think they have been wronged, usually by a government agency or one of the utility companies.

After a while, you start to think about the folks you would like to interview, and ask the questions you would like to ask. For example:

I really want to interview somebody who has written a book about the Kennedy assassination that says there was no conspiracy, that Lee Harvey Oswald acted alone, and that the Warren Commission report was absolutely true.

I want to hear somebody interviewed who says

that gold and silver are real bad investments and not a hedge against inflation and that we should all invest our money in formica.

Just one time, I want to hear some psychic say, "How should I know?"

I want to interview a movie producer who will say, "This is really a pretty dull movie, but I need the money and hope everyone will go see this piece of garbage anyway."

The interview I really want to do is with a doctor who says that potatoes are the most healthful food in the world, and the more you eat, the longer you live. When I find that doctor, not only will I buy his book, but I'll take that rascal to lunch and teach him how a real pro eats!

You Learn About Loneliness, Too

I guess I never really understood loneliness until I started to do a radio talk show. I thought I did, but what I had mistaken for loneliness was little league compared to what people go through on a day-to-day, hour-to-hour, minute-to-minute basis. I break it down this closely, because when a person is really in pain from loneliness, a minute can be a long time.

I still find it hard to accept that some people out there are so alone and in such pain that they will call a voice on the radio to try to get help or at least some conversation—even if it has to be from a stranger.

I have talked to numerous people who were really troubled, really in pain, and I think I can safely say that the majority, even the ones who were talking about suicide, were only about three or four hugs from being okay.

Funseekers, I've never preached to you, but don't let anyone you know get in that shape. Give them a hug. If there was more hugging going on, the psychiatrists would all be looking for work.

One of the best things about being on the radio is the nice people you meet. It's sort of like a little bonus to have people recognize you on the street or in a restaurant. I'd be the biggest liar in the world if I didn't admit that to be recognized is a real ego trip.

I love it when they come up and speak to me. Nice folks who just want to tell me that they enjoy what I do. I guess the comment I get most often is, "I listen every day, but I never call." I wish I could tell them all: "Hey, I love listeners when they call. It's a bonus."

I'll never forget the very excited man who came up to me and said, "Ludlow Porch! I never miss your show. I've been listening to you for years. Why, I've been listening to you since before you went on the air." That's a good trick!

A number of people have rushed up and said, "Boy, Ludlow, you're a big fan of mine!"

I never get tired of meeting them on or off the air, and I hope they know that they make it all possible. They are the most important people in radio: they are the audience.

A Fond and Gentle Look At the WHACKOS

I guess before I can tell you who the Whackos are, I should explain what a Whacko is.

I think a Whacko could be described as a person who sees humor in this old life and absolutely refuses to take himself too seriously.

A real Whacko thinks nothing is so serious that a little fun can't be poked at it. Whackos come in all shapes and sizes. They enjoy calling me on the air and for a few minutes being as outrageous as their own creativity will allow, and that's pretty creative.

They are my people, and oh, how I love them!

Beef Jerky

Beef was the original whacko. In real life he is a math teacher. He enjoys politics and sees the lunacy in the games that politicians play. I have often wished that Old Beef would run for public office. I think the country could laugh itself right into a healthy condition with Beef at the helm.

He values his privacy and never shows up at any of the Whacko functions, but when I answer the phone and hear his voice, I know that he is about to put some politician in his place.

I wish Beef Jerky would run for president.

Bloody Mary

Mary is a tax consultant in real life, and she really drinks as much as her name indicates. I guess when you make your living filling out income tax forms, you are entitled to a drink now and then, and, as we say down South, Mary is bad to drink.

She called me on the air on Thanksgiving and said she had a problem. She had made a mistake and basted her turkey with vodka, and the turkey kept opening the door and turning the heat down. If the U.S. had an Olympic drinking team, Bloody Mary would be the captain.

Homer Southwell

Homer is a Southern author who hates the North and everything about the North. Since he was first on my radio show, he has become something of a folk hero. People either love him or hate him; there is no middle ground with old Homer. Homer says things like: "For recreation I read the obituaries in the *New York Times*." "I wouldn't go North for a three-day orgy with Charlie's Angels." "The best form of birth control is a Bronx accent."

You can see that Homer is not a moderate when it comes to Yankees. His first book was *Yankee Go Home*. The sequel is *And Stay There*.

In real life, Homer is a super salesman with a charming personality and a penchant for dirty language, a love of good bourbon, and a sense of humor as big as his hometown of Bremen, Georgia.

Kitty Litter

Kitty is a dear heart who has a most beautiful

outlook on life. She lives in Tucker, Georgia, and is a Queen of the Annual Tucker Flipflop Parade. She is a lovely, crazy lady who makes Atlanta smile whenever she calls my show. In real life, Kitty sells real estate, and on Sunday she plays the organ at her church. If there were more folks like Kitty, nobody would ever frown again. Oh, how I love that funny, beautiful lady!

Greg Garni

Greg is the president-elect of the Parsley Preservation Society and as such is my arch-enemy, because everyone knows that parsley is bad for you. I have been trying for the last few years to wipe out parsley in our time, and of course Greg is pushing it as a cure-all. He always wears green and carries a picket sign that says "Porch is a Commie—Parsley cures warts." I hate to say it, but in real life Greg is one of my favorite people. He is a real-estate salesman with a personality that would make Conrad Hilton want to buy a house from him. If parsley ever becomes the national vegetable, you can bet your escrow it was Greg's doing.

Kid Chocolate

The Kid is a retired boxer who talks like a cross between Rocky Graziano and Amos and Andy. On the air he is loud, boisterous and very, very funny. In real life he works for the federal government. He is one of the greatest men I have ever known. He works with boys and girls who are in trouble and never seems to tire of helping kids. If it were not for Kid Chocolate, many children in Georgia would have no

Santa at Christmas. If it were in my power, Kid Chocolate would have a statue in his honor bigger than Grand Canyon.

Sgt. John Stryker

This Whacko takes his name from the character John Wayne played in *Sands of Iwo Jima*. You can bet when the topic of conversation comes around to patriotism, Sgt. Stryker will call—a funny, intelligent man who loves his country.

In real life he is an airline pilot and a lieutenant colonel in the Marine Corps Reserve.

When the Marines said they were looking for a few good men, they had Sgt. Stryker in mind.

M.T. Head

M.T. is Georgia's only auto mechanic and brain surgeon. He is a graduate of Shorty's Agricultural, Mechanical & Medical School (A, M & M), Pit Bar-B-Q Cafe and Truck Stop, Letohatchie, Alabama 36047.

M.T. may be one of the funniest men I have ever met. In real life he works for the government and is just as funny off the air as he is on. When it comes to making me laugh, M.T. has me under his thumb; a talented man who should replace Johnny Carson as host of the *Tonight Show*.

B.N. Towne

B.N. is the announcer not only for the Cordele 500 Stock Car Race, but also for the Great Southeastern Quarter Horse Jamboree and Pig Roast. I have never met anyone who tells a story better than B.N. In real life he is an insurance agent full time and a horse nut part time. He is a crazy Irishman who knows about life, and he enjoys every second of it. One hell of a man whose company I enjoy more than a trip to Six Flags.

Grits O'Malley

Grits O'Malley is insane. When you turn this man loose on radio, you never know what he is going to say because *he* never knows what he is going to say. But when he starts to spin tales about O'Malley International Airport, you just know that he's got to be on the FAA's list of Ten Least Wanted Men. In real life he is the comptroller for a carpet manufacturing company and a man I enjoy being with because, like all funny men, he smiles a lot.

The Bard of Avon

The Bard may be one of the most talented people I know. When he calls me on the air, you can bet that he has just written a piece of poetry that is going to have an effect on you; it may make you laugh, or it may make you cry, but it will always make you think.

In real life the Bard is retired and fills in as a volunteer in a local library.

The Bard's beloved wife died a few years ago, and her death was the biggest loss of his life. But out of his deep sorrow springs a love and understanding of his fellow man that I have never seen before. His poetry can be funny or sad, but it is always full of love and compassion.

When I grow up, I want to be just like the Bard.

Willie Mayhem, Roosevelt Capote, Murray the Singing Cowboy, Chung Foo, Rick Randell, Obediah Gillis.

These are just a few of the voices that have been done on my show by David Milford. David is an actor, and the times that we spent together as a team are special to me. Don't forget that name: David Milford. With the kind of talent he has, you can expect big things from him.

Bubba Martinez, Norman Sadly, Laverne Labonza, Clyde the Drunk, Jake Labonza, Dave Lockwood, Rollo Trumball, Bernard Fourquarts, Lucrecia, The Rev. Anthony Slatz.

The character of my friend Tom Deardorff comes out a little bit in some of the characters he created. Space does not permit the listing of all the Whackos that were and are Tom Deardorff. Tom thinks funny and enjoys putting the world on. When I am privileged to be in Tom's company, strange things usually happen.

There is just no way to write a description of all the Whackos—that would be a whole 'nother book—but I am going to try to list them. If I leave anybody out, I hope they understand that it's not a lack of love or admiration for their creativity, but just a slip of my memory.

Gladys Rountree
Scarlett O'Horowitz
Phenius Fourpanel
Bozo Roberts
Peg Leg

Rasslin' Willie
Philip T. Blanks
Lithonia
Montana Slim
Cowboy Bob
El Bado
Boom Boom
Shirley the Stripper
Wilbur
Bedpan Annie
The Midget
Leon McSleze
Al K. Hall
Justin Case
The Big Oak Tree
The Big Fig
Confusski
86
Alice the Computer
Bud Householder
Sadie Baby
Skates McFate
Elvis
Jerome the Sneezing Duck
The Ugly Guitar Player
Patton's Mama
Charlie the Check Chaser
Efus Pitch
The Knockout Kid
Drive-Off Kid
Marcel Bedwetter
Birmingham
Dawn

The Coffee Lady
Dolly
Storm Troop
Radish Rose
Leidus Ruin
Tal
Buck
The Roswell Traveling Salesman
Big Al
The Football Referee
Bones
Snellville Friend
Billy Bob Moody
Count Dracula
Hard-Hearted Hannah
Roll Tide
Chas the Handyman
Barney Oldfellow
Left-Handed Jai Alai Player
Freddie Lisp
Phonebone
Settee Davenport
The Old Grouch
Boom Boom Town
Ghost Town
Gomer
Aunt Bea
Otis
Baby Cakes
Sky
Big Daddy from Tucker
Talmadge Scruggs
Dusty Attic

The Artful Dodger
Lulu
The Athlete's Foot
Bat Guano
The Weekend Politician
Emory Board
Rosie
The Southern Gentleman
Chas. S. Limburger
Collard S. Ginsberg
Big Jim & Shirley
Weeping Willow
The Swamp Lady
The Red Ryder
Cowboy Trivia Player
Shelf Head
Tar Heel
The Poet Laureate of Mableton
Harry S. Northbest
The Appliance Salesman
Truman
The Wire-Mouthed Lady
The Lavender Kid
Steve Lance
Salty
Sarge
El Cheapo
Lou Ann Poovey
Billy Jean
Bee Bop
Arthur T. Ritis
Pneumonia
Esmeralda Jackson

Earline Bountiful
Ralph Raindrop
313
Nudie White
The Phantom
Jimmy the Pres
Lucille
The Blue Plate Psychic
Southern Comfort
The German Lady
The School Teacher
Leland Picket
Blanche

A Great Way to Make a Living

When you do a talk radio show five days a week, you are prepared to have a lot of peaks and valleys. There are days when you can do no wrong; the topic you have chosen to talk about is burning up the phone lines, or your guest is as sharp as a King Hardware pocket knife.

Then there are those days when nothing seems to be going well. Your sure-fire topic is going down for the third time. It's you against the world, and your only weapons are a microphone and your wits.

I remember the day I was sure my topic was perfect. I introduced it and was all set for the switchboard to melt down under the volume of calls I knew would come.

Nothing happened. I mean, *nothing.* I gave it my best shot and tried for about ten minutes to drum up some interest in my topic; still no response.

I went to a commercial and came back with a brand-new topic. Same result: no calls. Another commercial, another topic, still no calls. I finally decided it was time to take the bull by the horns, or whatever you take a bull by. I said, "Okay, you people. I have introduced three dynamite topics— topics that would get good response anywhere in the world. I know how to do a talk show, so it ain't me. It's you. Now, I'm going to ask you to call one more time, and if I have to come out there and slap hell out of fifteen or twenty of you, the next time I tell you to call, you'll call!"

The switchboard lit up like a wino at a tasting party. If begging doesn't help, threaten.

This kind of thing rarely happens. I would be less than honest if I didn't admit that I have one of the best jobs in the world. To be able to make a living doing something that is as much fun as my job is almost sinful. Not only do I get to talk about things that interest me, but I meet some wild and wonderful people. Where else can you sit down and talk to the likes of Charlton Heston, Andy Griffith, and Mercedes McCambridge and get paid for it?

In the last seven years, I have:

Been invited to Fiji by Raymond Burr.
Had my hand kissed by Van Johnson.
Got drunk with Pat Paulsen.
Had by belly patted by Cloris Leachman.
Been insulted by Shelly Berman.
Insulted Lee Majors.
Had a Swedish massage by Gunilla Knudsen.
Talked Southern with Andy Griffith.
Had dinner with John Gary.
Ridden a freight elevator with Mel Torme.
Smoked a cigar with E.G. Marshall.
Talked about old-time radio with Don Ameche.
Kissed Gloria DeHaven smack in the mouth.
Laughed at Sam Levenson.
Marveled at Rich Little.
Been embarrassed by Paul Lynde.

Played pass-the-bottle with Forrest Tucker.
Made Don Knotts nervous.
Waited for Bob Hope to go to the bathroom.
Had a cheeseburger with Peter Breck.
Fallen in love with Myrna Loy.
Talked baseball with Ted Williams.
Eaten barbecue with Godfrey Cambridge.
Had John Gary sing in my living room.
Kissed Claude Akins' mama.
Gotten a vitamin from Bob Cummings.
Talked about Sid Caesar with Imogene Coca.
Talked about Imogene Coca with Sid Caesar.
Set up a blind date for Barbara Eden.

You have to admit one thing, funseekers—it's a
great way to make a living!

Universal Truths?

Not All Old Sayings Are Wise

Have you ever stopped to think about all the wise old sayings we hear every day that just don't make sense at all? We grow up with them, and after hearing them over and over, we accept them as gospel, but when we stop to examine them up close, they fall apart.

Take, for example, the wise old saying, "Be nice to everybody you meet on the way up, because you meet the same people on the way down." That's dumb. Common sense will tell you that you meet an entirely different group of folks on your way down.

We are taught all our lives that divorce is a horrible thing, and I don't guess anyone would argue that. But at the same time we are taught to rectify our mistakes.

From early childhood, we are told to clean our plates. Then, as adults, we are told that overeating will lead to an early grave.

How about this one: "A penny saved is a penny earned." Try that one next time your teenager wants $100 to rent a tux for the junior-senior.

And don't forget this one: "A whistling girl and a crowing hen always come to no good end." Now, that's just not true. Take Big Red Hensley. She whistles all the time, and everybody knows that not only is she probably the best waitress anywhere, but she owns the biggest truck stop in Heard County.

You know, sometimes children hear all these old sayings, and I know they must just get sick to death of them.

When something comes out of the mouths of babes, you ought to listen. Like the time my son Phil was about seven years old. He was not very hungry and had not eaten all of his dinner. He asked permission to leave the table, with about three-fourths of his plate of food still uneaten.

His mother looked real upset, and said, "Phil, children in China are starving to death."

Phil said, "That's okay, Mama. They're Communists."

Try to keep a stern face after that one!

Early to Rise Will Wear You Out

All my life I've heard, "Early to bed, early to rise, makes a man healthy, wealthy, and wise." It's one of those clichés that sounds so good that you take it as gospel and never question it.

But if you pull the feathers off and take a close look, you can quickly see that this particular cliché holds less water than a roll of chicken wire.

Let's take the case of Thomas Edison. History tells us that he would go days at a time without going to bed. He would take little catnaps wherever he was, never take his clothes off, and never go near a bed for a week or more. Sounds to me like he might have gotten a little gamy, but I don't guess that stops you from being an inventor.

Say what you wish about Edison's personal hygiene, the old boy invented about everything there is except maybe the wheel, the switchblade knife, and well water.

Not only did he not go to bed *early*, he didn't go to bed at *all* most of the time. I don't know how healthy he was, but he lived a right long life, as I recall. He was certainly wealthy by any standards, and he was wise, as his works tell.

The point I'm trying to make is that getting up early is just not all it's cracked up to be.

Some people just do not function well early. I happen to be one of those people. As a matter of fact, my heart absolutely refuses to hit a lick till about 10:15 every morning. But still the legend of early rising being good continues to live. The fanatics say things like "the early bird gets the worm." That's okay if you like worms.

I can tell you, funseekers, after doing an early morning radio show for a year and getting up every day at 4:30 A.M., I came to one inescapable conclusion:

If a sunrise was so great, the Lord would have had it happen around 3:30 in the afternoon, so more folks could see it.

How to Tell a Redneck From a Country Boy

Ignorance is like concrete; once it stays there awhile, it's awfully tough to get rid of.

Now, I don't mind a fellow being a little ignorant, because in most cases, if he'll listen to somebody who knows, he can learn and no longer be ignorant, unless of course he's stupid in the first place, in which case there's not much you can do for him except not hang out with him, because you naturally don't want folks to think you are ignorant enough to hang out with somebody stupid.

A friend of mine recently said he didn't know the difference between a redneck and a country boy. And it occurred to me that there is a lot of ignorance on this subject. So if you'll listen carefully, I'll tell you the difference, and you will no longer be as ignorant as you were, unless of course, you're stupid, in which case you're probably reading a Daffy Duck comic book right now.

A redneck usually has a tattoo. A country boy would never have a tattoo, 'cause his mama would have a running fit.

A redneck's favorite drink is beer. A country boy's favorite drink is a big orange.

A redneck talks a lot about smoking dope. A country boy thinks only dopes smoke.

A redneck hates policemen. A country boy hopes his son will grow up to be one.

A redneck will say something bad about a country boy's mama. A country boy will take a redneck out in the parking lot and break both his legs for saying something bad about his mama.

A redneck thinks bread is something you spend. A country boy thinks it's something you pour syrup on.

I really hope you have been paying attention. You need to keep this straight, and I'll tell you why: any time you confuse a redneck and a country boy, you make 'em both mad. Besides, we all need to fight ignorance wherever we find it. That's the main reason we vote.

Fat People of the World, Unite!

I'm giving serious consideration to starting a brand new organization. I'm going to call it the N.A.A.F.P. That stands for the National Association for the Advancement of Fat People.

Arise, tubbies of the world! We no longer have to take the abuse and rip-offs put upon us by the emaciated majority. Do you realize that you can't pick up a magazine or a newspaper without seeing some advertisement trying to take your money on the pretense of taking off weight?

The headlines jump out at you: TAKE THIS $9.99 CAPSULE AND IN JUST 90 DAYS YOU'LL BE UP TO YOUR ARMPITS IN BEAUTIFUL BLONDES! Or how about this one: JOIN OUR GROUP. WE MEET ONCE A WEEK, SING SONGS, HEAR LECTURES, AND MAKE LIGHT OF THE POOR DUMB GLUTTONS WHO DIDN'T LOSE ANY WEIGHT LAST WEEK.

And how about the health spas? Let me tell you something, funseekers; the only way you are going to lose any weight at a health spa is if you get your leg torn off in one of those machines that were designed by an evil scientist for the specific purpose of causing a hernia.

No. There is only one answer: the lardoes of the

world must band together, vote as a bloc, and declare once and for all that this is the year of the pork chop. We must demand our rights. I have long felt that if we're going to have any law and order in this country, the first thing we have to do is break every mirror we come across. Any adult male weighing less than two hundred pounds must be tracked down and force-fed mashed potatoes until he makes Orson Welles look like Marie Osmond.

Realize one thing, funseekers: Fat is where it's at.

Hitler was skinny, and look what a quarrelsome old boy he was. On the other hand, Santa Claus will go about two hundred and forty, not counting his Ho-Ho's.

And never forget the motto of the N.A.A.F.P.: "There's nothing neat about seeing your feet."

I know not what course others may take, but I for one stand with Patrick Henry, who said . . .

"More gravy, Leon."

Computers Are Not the Warmest Friends

I guess we are lucky that the computer age is here. If you examine it closely, you will see that by and large it has really made our lives easier. Thanks to the computer, we were able to put Americans on the moon, and almost everyone can remember the national pride we felt when Neil Armstrong took that first step on the lunar surface.

And of course the computer has been a great step forward for medical science.

But like everything else, you've got to take the good with the bad, like when a computer fouls up your water or power bill, and you can't find a human anywhere in the company to correspond with about it.

I guess everybody has heard about the computers they have put outside banks now. They are really nice. If you need some cash after the bank closes, you just go by and put your card in the computer, punch in your secret number, and a little screen lights up and tells you what your balance is. Or you can make deposits or withdrawals, and just about do all your banking at night.

When these computers first came out, the banks wanted everybody to use them, so they started to advertise about these "instant" all-night machines.

The first one was called The Instant Banker, and then they thought it would be more personal if they gave the computers names. So one bank came out with Tillie the All-Time Teller, and another bank called its computer Buddy.

I live kinda out of town, and my bank was about the last one to get instant all-night tellers. But I was sure glad to get my card in the mail. It was called Maurice, the Money Man, and boy! was I proud to get my Maurice card.

I went down to the bank to take out some money the first night, just to see how it worked.

I put my Maurice card in and punched my magic number. The little screen lighted up and said, "Hey, Luddy. How's your mama 'n 'em?"

I punched in, "Not bad, Maurice. How you been?"

"Fine, thanks. Can I hep you?"

I punched in that I wanted to take out $200.

Maurice lighted up and said, "What you trying to pull, fat boy? You ain't had a $200 balance in your life. Shove off or I'll call a cop!"

I should have known there ain't no way to have a meaningful relationship with a computer.

The world is full of old, old mysteries that seem to defy solution. I'm not talking about things like flying saucers or ghosts. I'm talking about the great *old* mysteries that folks are still working on. Like whatever happened to Amelia Earhart? Did she really crash on Saipan and fall into the hands of the Japanese? Does Bigfoot really exist, and is he now roaming the Northwest?

And what about the most famous of all, the Loch Ness monster? He (or maybe they) has been seen and reported by generations around the lake, and scientists have tried everything from sonar to submarines to capture it. But so far, no monster, and very little hard evidence of the monster's existence.

And how about all those ships and planes that have disappeared in the Bermuda Triangle?

The mysteries go on and on. More research, more rumors, more books—and no solution.

Take, for example, the mystery of Hogan's goat.

Legend tells us that Rufus Hogan was the sole owner of a large, unattractive billy goat. Rufus was a bachelor, and the only thing in the world he held in high regard was his billy goat. He spent all his time with that goat and loved him like a son.

Rufus was expelled from five churches because

the congregations would not tolerate the presence of the goat.

All his friends abandoned Rufus because of his association with the goat and his insistence on carrying the animal everywhere he went.

One day the blamed goat turned up missing. Legend has it that Hogan looked for him night and day for years. Then one day he found the goat living in sin with a nanny goat of questionable virtue. Hogan went berserk, and in his grief and anger he killed them both.

Well, legend tells us that Hogan was never punished for his crime; as a matter of fact, he now runs a profitable chain of barbecue restaurants.

And that, funseekers, is the legend of Hogan's goat. And if you believe that one, I've got some stock in a hula-hoop factory I want to sell you.

Denominational Cooking

I guess we all have a special area of expertise. No matter how limited you think your talent may be, somewhere you have an area of expertise. You may know more about soap operas than any lady south of Peyton Place, or you may know how to raise African violets or how to play a bagpipe.

I guess the point I'm trying to make is that everybody is an expert on something.

Take me, for instance. I don't like to brag, but I am probably the foremost expert in the world on denominational cooking. Now, I know what you're thinking: What is denominational cooking? Well, quite simply put, that is the ability to tell someone's religious persuasion simply by eating some food they have prepared.

This is not an ability that is easily come by. You must spend many sunny afternoons at all-day singings and dinner on the grounds. You must taste each dish carefully and make mental notes. Once this has been done, you soon learn some gastronomic truisms. Like, if you want to get good string beans you must go to a Methodist dinner on the grounds. The Methodists are far and away the best string-bean cooks on the face of the earth.

On the other hand, if you want fried chicken the

way God intended, then you must eat it prepared by a Baptist. Nobody can fry a chicken like a Baptist.

A few more facts that you may find useful: Church of Christ members tend to serve corn bread, while Presbyterians almost always lean toward rolls. Catholic food tends to be spicy, and Episcopalians are particularly adept at hams and roasts.

The common denominator seems to be the iced tea. They almost all like it sweetened. I can therefore reach only one conclusion: If you like your tea unsweetened, you better get right with the Lord, 'cause on the evidence in question I tend to think you're in a bunch of trouble.

It's Time for a New Fad

If you keep a close eye on the calendar, you'll notice that about every ten years a new fad comes along that absolutely sweeps the country.

In the twenties, for reasons known to particularly nobody, college students started to eat goldfish. I don't know whether they were suffering from a lack of protein or if their brains were all slick, but nonetheless, thousands of folks were doing it. The Lord knows that I'm in favor of eating fish, but I like them fried and with hush puppies.

Do you remember phone-booth stuffing? This was where a group of folks got together to see how many people could get into one phone booth. It didn't accomplish much, but you did get to know some folks a *lot* better.

Let's not forget flagpole sitting. This was where you climbed to the top of a flagpole to see how long you could stay there.

You didn't do anything; you just sat there. Doesn't that sound exciting?

Well, in case you haven't noticed, funseekers, we have a new fad that just may be sillier than all the rest. Here's the way this lunacy works: the first thing you do is buy a very expensive pair of what we used to call tennis shoes. Then you put on some type of silly costume. It can be a pair of sweat pants with shorts on the outside, or you can wear cut-off jeans and a T-shirt with the sleeves cut out. It doesn't matter exactly what the costume is, as long as it's silly looking.

Once you get all outfitted, you run. That's all; you just run. I know what you're asking. Where do you run *to*?

Well, funseekers, you don't run to anywhere. You just run.

I asked one runner, "Why do you run? If you got to be someplace in a hurry, I'll let you use my car."

He said, "I don't have to be anywhere. I run to make my pulse beat faster."

I said, "Here, have a cigarette. It'll do the same thing."

I think it's time for a new fad, and I mean one that makes some sense. How about if we all start doing more rockin' and starin'? You just sit down in a rocking chair and stare.

Now, that wouldn't accomplish anything, either, but think of the money you could save on tennis shoes.

Movies Aren't Better Than Ever

When television started to catch on in the early fifties, the folks who really felt the pinch were the movie makers. They almost went down the tube as Uncle Miltie danced across the TV screen every Tuesday night.

Hollywood got into high gear and came up with all kinds of gimmicks from 3-D to Cinerama to Todd-AO.

But nothing seemed to help; movie houses across the country were closing right and left. It soon became apparent that folks would not go out to see what they could see at home.

Well, the folks in Hollywood solved their financial problem by making movies with a lot of cussing and a lot of skin. The formula worked; now theaters are packing them in seven days a week.

But that's not what I want to talk about. When things looked the darkest for Hollywood, they came out with a slogan to try to help business. The slogan was "Movies Are Better Than Ever."

Well, the simple fact of the matter is, they ain't.

Have they been able to replace any of the greats like Cagney, Gable, Bogart, and Garfield? Compare this crowd with Beatty, Hoffman, Pacino, and Redford. Get the picture? Same business, but the difference is like daylight and dark. What actor on the scene today could replace Gable as Rhett Butler? What actor on the scene today could go to the chair with the arrogance of Cagney? Picture Robert Redford playing the part of Fred C. Dobbs in *The Treasure of Sierra Madre*.

Can you imagine Dustin Hoffman storming up Mt. Suribachi instead of John Wayne?

Yes, sir. I sure miss them. I miss them all. Edward G. Robinson, Gene Autry, Donald O'Connor, Peggy Ryan, Charles Laughton, Lash LaRue, Whip Wilson, Eddie Dean, Fred Astaire, Chester Morris, Sonja Henie.

I miss Johnny Weissmuller and Greer Garson. I miss the Sons of the Pioneers and Edward Everett Horton.

This new crowd of actors just ain't never going to make it. Just remember—you heard it from the same guy who predicted the ballpoint pen would never catch on.

Times Do Change

The world has changed so much in the last fourteen or fifteen years that I hardly recognize it anymore.

People are saying and doing strange things, and for the most part, it's darned hard to keep up with it. For example, first the Chinese were our friends and everybody knew it. Then you look around and they are our enemies. You no more than get used to not liking them when you read in the paper that they are our friends again, and to prove it they show the president on TV drinking liquor with a bunch of Chinese. Say what you want to about Richard Nixon, only a fool would drink with his enemies.

Yes, sir. Life is sure confusing. They have changed the War Department to the Defense Department, and they have changed "personality" to "charisma."

You look around one day and find that all of a sudden there are plenty of buffaloes but the railroads are almost extinct. It's really hard to figure out what is going on, no matter how hard you work at it. It just gets more and more confusing.

There is something really lying heavy on my mind that I've been trying to figure out. When I first heard about it, it hit me hard enough to knock the teeth out of a sausage grinder. It's about this man who was running for president. He went all over the country making speeches and trying to get folks to vote for him. He bought a lot of stuff on credit like TV ads, bumper stickers, buttons. He threw a few barbecues and ran up a multi-million-dollar campaign debt.

It seems that he and a bunch of his cronies are giving fund-raising dinners and getting donations to try to pay back all the money.

But that isn't what's bothering me; what is bothering me is, how was he gonna pay back all that money if he *had* been elected?

It's an interesting question. But come to think of it, I don't think I really want to know the answer, because I just know it would depress me.

Things I Know Nothing About

I have a sign over my desk that says, "There has been an alarming increase in the number of things I know nothing about." I put the sign there as a joke, but it's not so funny when you realize how true it is.

I may be wrong, but it seems to me that the more I read, the less I understand.

Take, for example, the national budget. As far as I know, everybody agrees that it would be a good thing to balance the national budget; but nobody seems willing just to go ahead and do it. I don't understand that.

I don't understand how the electoral college works, or why we need it. Seems to me that the fella that gets the most votes ought to get the job.

I don't understand what Ralph Nader does for a living.

I don't understand why, if front-wheel-drive vehicles are so good, we didn't have them years ago.

I don't understand why the U.S. stays in the U.N. I can't recall the U.N.'s accomplishing anything. I mean, we wound up in Korea and Vietnam while we were all paid up in our dues. If the U.N. can't solve anything, what good is it?

I don't understand why old beer cans last forever, and new cans rust out.

I don't understand Laverne and Shirley.

I don't understand how Orson Bean makes a living.

I don't understand what makes the Chinese such good ping pong players.

I don't understand how preachers can play golf, 'cause it makes me cuss a lot.

I don't understand folks who drink Scotch. I've tried it. It tastes bad.

Yes, sir, there has been an alarming increase in the number of things I know nothing about.

It Doesn't Take Any Time to Hum

I have been accused of living in the past, and to that charge I plead guilty; it's true that I miss a lot of things that have fallen victim to the passing parade. Things like rumble seats, prom parties, and Skinny Ennis.

But there are a lot of other things I miss that are less tangible.

For example, have you noticed that people don't hum anymore? Now, I know that's not a big thing, but I sure do miss it. And I can't figure for the life of me what happened to the hummers of the world. I know that the pace of our day-to-day existence has quickened, but it doesn't take any time to hum.

I can remember like it was yesterday my grandmother humming as she worked around the kitchen. She would only hum church hymns. Her favorite was "When the Roll is Called Up Yonder, I'll Be There."

Mr. Moody was also a hummer. You remember Mr. Moody. He owned Moody's Shoe Shop, and you could wait while he fixed your shoes and at the same time be serenaded by his humming.

In addition to the hummers of the world vanishing, I think whistling is a vanishing art. When was the last time you heard somebody going about daily tasks and whistling at the same time? If you know someone who whistles, you'd better enjoy it, because it is a vanishing art.

I think I've about figured out what happened to the hummers and whistlers of the world. I thought for a while they were just too busy, but now I think that folks are just not as happy as they used to be.

Ain't it a shame that folks don't smile as much as they used to? 'Cause sunshine is very good for your teeth.

Comfort Has Many Faces

Love Means . . .

I can't remember if Ryan O'Neal said it or if Ali MacGraw said it. It doesn't make any difference, but one of them looked at the other and said, "Love means never having to say you're sorry."

I want you to think about that—"Love means never having to say you're sorry."

That is probably the dumbest thing I have ever heard. The simple fact of the matter is, it has nothing to do with love one way or the other.

The folks who write love songs and books are as fouled up as Hogan's goat. Let me give you a few examples.

How about this one: "You always hurt the one you love."

On the face of it, you know that is not true; sometimes you hurt folks that you don't love.

Or how about that famous song that says "You don't have to say you love me, just be close at hand." Whoever wrote that has dumb oozing out of every pore.

I sometimes think that the people who write love songs are single and have never been in love, because they have a hard time capturing exactly what love is.

Let me tell you the kinds of songs I wish they'd write about love.

Love is sitting up together all night in the hospital waiting room praying to God the doctor can break the baby's fever.

Love is fixing her favorite meal when you are as tired as she is.

Love is the feeling you get watching your son get his first haircut.

Love is when she walks by your chair and touches the top of your head.

Love is when you enjoy her beating you at Scrabble.

Love is looking into her eyes while Sinatra sings "Yesterday."

Love is the smell of baby powder.

Love is bringing her flowers when it's not a special occasion.

Love is enjoying watching her sleep.

Love doesn't mean never having to say you're sorry; it means being able to say you're sorry and mean it.

Barbara

The first time we met was at the United States Marine Corps Air Station at Cherry Point, North Carolina.

She was twenty minutes old and I was twenty years old. As far as I was concerned, it was love at first sight. She was as beautiful then as she is now.

She had great amounts of jet black hair, and even then she smiled a lot.

The first time I got to hold her was January 19, 1954. We were leaving the hospital; she was all wrapped up in blankets; it was raining softly. A nurse stopped us on the sidewalk and asked to see her. A drop of rain hit her nose, and I heard her cry for the first time, standing there in the rain. The first time she had felt rain, and I was there.

Her first tooth came through, in the middle on the bottom. I saw it when I was giving her a bottle. It was beautiful.

The first step she took was from her mother to me. We all three laughed like she had just won an Olympic gold medal.

When she was three, she had to have surgery. She was so brave. I went into the bathroom at Georgia Baptist Hospital and cried.

When the surgery was over, she was fine, and I cried again.

I took her to the nursery for the first time. I felt guilty because her mother had to go to work to help me make it through school. She enjoyed it and the "Kiddy Ranch" fairly glowed because she was there, always laughing, always running and asking more questions than any four-year-old in history.

Her first-grade teacher told me she was a bright child; I felt that was a gross understatement.

One day she told me she wanted to play softball. I watched her over the next few seasons while she went from an awkward child to a fine athlete, a catcher that Yogi Berra would have been proud of. She loved it. I loved her, so I loved it, too.

I never understood or shared her love for the Beatles, but when Santa came I made sure that John, Paul, George, and Ringo were in Santa's sack—albums and records and posters and sofa pillows picturing them in all their long-haired glory.

Her first date was with a young boy who, like the Beatles, had no forehead. I hated him, not for any particular reason, but because he was part of a growing-up process that instinct told me to fight with my last breath.

When she got her senior ring I knew the fight was almost over, that the calendar and mother nature were going to win. Coming in a graceful second was the best I could hope for.

She had wanted to be a nurse ever since Santa had brought her a doctor's kit, complete with stethoscope and red cinnamon pills.

When she walked up on that stage, she was a

student; when she walked down, she was a nurse. I cried again.

There was a time when we were apart.

In my ignorance and pride I had objected to the man she had chosen for a husband. Looking back now, I wonder if any man could have satisfied my requirements.

In my mind she was perfect. Therefore, any man worthy of her had to be perfect, too.

I didn't go to her wedding, a dumb, thoughtless act of a man with too much pride. I had been defied by someone who had never defied me before. I was so wrong, so very, very wrong. I had brought her sorrow—sorrow that she had not earned and did not deserve.

I did not see or hear from her for several empty, lonely months. One day quite by accident I ran into her at my mother's house. There was no exchange of words. I took her in my arms. We cried, we hugged. She had forgiven me, and her love brought the sunshine back into my life.

The first time I saw my granddaughter was when they were pushing her down the hall in an incubator. I made them stop so I could see her.

While I was standing there looking at that beautiful, wiggly baby, I'm not really sure I saw her because my mind rushed back to a raindrop on a baby's nose in 1954. I thought of how beautiful and perfect she was. I remembered her first night of trick or treat. I remembered the first time she sat on a department store Santa's lap. I remembered "Kiddy Ranch," the first grade, the tooth fairy. I remembered training wheels, the Beatles, and her cheerleader's uniform. I remembered the senior ring, a boy I didn't like, and helping her study to get her driving license. I remembered teaching her how to say her prayers, how to hold a softball bat, and to always say yes ma'am and no ma'am. I remembered the Sunday school certificates, the crisp white nurse's uniform and the pride I have always felt for her.

She's grown now, and I can't warm her bottle or buy her ice cream. And I can't get all the other thrills I used to, but when she calls and I pick up the phone and I hear her say, "Hi, Daddy!," suddenly I'm twenty years old and she is twenty minutes old.

I pray to God that never changes.

I promised my son Phil that I would mention him in this book.

Hush, I'm Squeakin'

There are many milestones in our lives, and most of them we are able to handle pretty easily. It seems that for every big decision we have to make, some way or the other the Lord always provides someone to give us some advice to get us over the hump.

When you are finally able to afford your first car, your dad or older brother is there to look at it with you or drive it around the block, and just give you some good, old-fashioned advice to make sure you come out of the deal all right.

The same is true when you decide to get married. Lord knows, there are plenty of people around with volumes of advice once you decide that you are ready to hit the center aisle with the girl of your dreams.

Then when it's time for the first home of your own, everybody is willing and able to tell you the great delights of being a homeowner; the insurance man is there to take care of your insurance needs; the exterminator handles all of your termites; and, of course, the real estate salesperson holds your hand all the way.

Then when your first baby comes along, you don't worry about that at all, because deep down you know that your wife, her mother, your mother, and the doctor know more about having babies than Snow White knew about dwarfs.

But there comes a time, funseekers, when you must go it alone. I am at a crossroads in my life, faced with a decision that only I can make.

I'm trying to buy a rocking chair for my porch, and the responsibility is awesome. Nobody can help me. I must do it alone. It is too personal to share with anyone.

I've spent weeks trying to get this right.

I found one that fits me real good, and I found one that is exactly the right style for my front porch, but I simply cannot find a rocking chair with the right squeak. They either squeak too much, or they don't squeak enough, and if you know anything at all about rocking chairs, you know that the squeak must be just right.

If the squeak is right, you can put up with a lot of other things. You can stand having a style that's not just right, or you can even have a bit of discomfort, but the squeak must be right.

Now, the reason the squeak is so hard to get right is because you need to test it on your front porch, and what's more, you need to test it at night. If you're not particular about your lifestyle, you can slide by with a substandard squeak in the daytime, but when you're sitting on that front porch at night and the only sounds you can hear are the crickets and an occasional katydid, then and only then does your rocking chair squeak become more important than the Magna Carta. You know, it makes you wonder where Ralph Nader is when you really need him.

I guess I'm oversimplifying this, but it seems a mystery to me that we can put a man on the moon, but we can't get a uniform rocking-chair-squeak law passed.

Daddy

I called him Daddy, though he wasn't really my father. But since my father died when I was less than two years old, he was the only Daddy I ever knew. He was my grandfather. When my mother was widowed in 1936, she had little choice but to take me home to her parents, where we lived for the rest of the happiest childhood God ever blessed a child with.

I was the only grandchild at that time, so there were long wonderful hours that I could spend with Daddy.

He was a small man, about five feet seven. But more love, humor, and compassion were packed into that body than any man's I've known before or since.

Sundays were very special to Daddy and me, because that was the only day he had off from work. After church he would take me by the hand and walk the four or five blocks to Glover's Pharmacy where I could have any flavor of ice cream I wanted. Then we'd walk down to the park, and he would push me in a swing while I licked away at my ice cream cone.

We'd get home just in time for one of my grandmother's Sunday dinners, and after dinner, Daddy would make his specialty—a huge pitcher of fresh-squeezed lemonade. Then the whole family, including aunts and uncles, would sit around on the front porch and drink lemonade and enjoy each other's company.

I never heard my grandfather say a harsh word about another human being. I never heard him curse except once when he was using a hand crank on his A Model and it kicked him.

My grandmother was an auburn-haired Scotch-Irish lady with a temper as quick as lightning, but I never heard a cross word—no, not one—between her and Daddy.

Daddy died in 1941, when I was six years old. It's been a very, very long time, but not a day goes by that I don't miss the pleasure of his company.

Hush and Pray

My grandmother was the most independent woman I ever knew. She was a native of Rock Hill, South Carolina. She had red hair and was proud of the Scottish blood that pumped through her veins. She was a gentle, loving lady who never spoke to a child but once to correct it. Her children were her life. She loved them with all her heart, but when they needed to be whacked, there was no hesitation. I called her Mama.

Her great ambition was for all of her children to get good educations and grow up to be ladies and gentlemen.

She used to say, "Get a good education, sonny boy. Once you have it, no one can ever take it away from you."

I remember one time the school principal sent a note home that said the next time Tommy talked in school, he was going to spank him. The first thing Mama did was to spank Tommy for bringing home a note about his conduct.

Then she called the principal and explained to him that she was the only person who could whip her children, and if he ever put the weight of his hand on one of hers, she would take the school apart brick by brick.

Spanking her children was not something to be delegated, according to Mama.

She was not afraid of anything that moved, with one exception: she was absolutely terrified of lightning.

I can remember very clearly when a thunderstorm would start, and the lightning was popping. She would take me to her big four-poster bed, where we would get under the cover, and she would pull the cover up over our heads.

During one storm I said, "Mama, why are we in bed? The lightning can strike us here, too."

She said, "Hush, sonny boy. Hush and pray."

It is kind of funny, the marks we carry from childhood.

No. I'm not afraid of lightning, but when things get really bad for me, and I'm convinced that it's not worth the struggle, I just close my eyes and I can hear Mama say, "Hush, sonny boy. Hush and pray."

Everybody has a list of favorite things. Here are some things I find important:

1. A town with a square and a courthouse in the middle.
2. Church bells.
3. Short sermons when you're hungry.
4. Brother Dave Gardner.
5. All-day singing and dinner on the grounds.
6. The Georgia Bulldogs and the Florida Gators on a Saturday afternoon in Jacksonville.
7. Fireplaces
8. Babies who smell like baby powder.
9. Frank Sinatra singing it slow.
10. A mailman who walks around his route, and you know him by name.
11. Edgar Buchanan.
12. The smell of leaves burning.
13. Johnny Weissmuller as Tarzan.
14. Glenn Miller records.
15. Clark Gable movies.
16. High school bands.
17. Mickey Spillane books.

18. An old man whittling.
19. Johnny Cash.
20. Walking in the rain.
21. Elections.
22. Oyster stew on a cold night.
23. Christmas.
24. The hole where a parking meter once was.
25. A soft drink box where you take the drinks out of ice-cold water.
26. A well with a bucket and dipper.
27. A ninety-yard touchdown.
28. The quiet beauty of new snow.
29. Basil Rathbone as Sherlock Holmes.
30. Ladies who still wear aprons around the house.
31. Old Glory blowing in the wind.
32. A young girl giggling.
33. Twenty miles to the gallon.
34. Holding her hand.

**Growing Up
Is Hard Work**

Some Jokes Aren't Funny

In the past few years, it has become popular to tell ethnic jokes. Everyone laughs, and it is all great fun. We tell jokes about Poles and Jews, about Blacks having natural rhythm or loving watermelon, about the Scotsman who is stingy, and about the Irishman who drinks too much. There are Catholic jokes and jokes about Baptist preachers.

If you are not the butt of the story, the joke is funny.

In all honesty, I must admit that I tell ethnic jokes. If the jokes are funny and not cruel, not only do I like to tell them, but I like to hear them.

I only draw the line on one kind of joke. I don't like to hear jokes about people with handicaps.

For example, I don't like to hear jokes about folks who stutter, and there must be about ten thousand jokes about stutterers. I'm here to tell you that I've heard them all, and I never have thought they were funny in the least. I never laugh, because I remember a little boy with a stutter. I remember how he felt when he couldn't say a word without stuttering and somebody always laughed at him. I remember when this boy stood in line at the Varsity and ordered something he didn't want because he couldn't say "two hotdogs all the way" without stuttering. I remember the terrible pain he felt in a Presbyterian Sunday School class because he couldn't say the Lord's Prayer without stuttering, and the Sunday School teacher accused him of not knowing it because he was too ashamed of his stuttering to try to say it.

I remember the agony this little boy grew up with.

I should. Because his name is Ludlow Porch.

There's a Time and Place For All-Out Fear

The other day I was reading a book by a psychologist. It was pretty much a stereotyped positive-thinking book. I guess we have all read one like it at one time or another.

It said all the things that they all say. I sometimes get the feeling that all you need to do to write a book on positive thinking is to read a book on positive thinking and then change the clichés around.

Norman Vincent Peale started it all with his *Power of Positive Thinking*. Since then, I guess a couple of hundred have been written, some good, and a lot very, very bad.

I was doing real well with this book and enjoying it until I got to the part about raising children. The yoyo who wrote this book said you must teach your children that there is no need for fear. He said fear is a state of mind, and nothing can hurt you that you won't allow to hurt you.

Now, a man who would say that is dumb enough to try to breed two sows. Say what you want about fear, but fear is necessary—there are a lot of things out there that will get you. Things like snakes (I mean *all* snakes) and things like sharks. If you aren't careful, the IRS will get you. If you don't believe me, ask Al Capone.

Auto mechanics will get you. If you don't believe that, then you ain't never had car trouble. Bumper jacks will get you. Sometimes even a zipper will get you.

Yes, sir. You can learn a lot from positive thinking books, but when you start to pass along what you have learned to your children, you be sure and tell them there are things out there that will get you, and when that happens, throw away your positive thinking book and remember what Sgt. Murphy said:

"When danger is all around you, and there is no way out, remember brave men get buried—wise men get exercise."

Shirley

I'll never forget the first time I saw Shirley. I just knew that she had to be the most beautiful girl that ever lived. Yes, sir. Right there in that seventh-grade class, old Cupid paid me his first visit.

Shirley was just perfect. She had long black hair that was always combed just right. She had big brown eyes that made the Hope diamond look like a Woolworth zircon. When she laughed, it sounded like a combination of branch water running over rocks and a Johnny Mathis record.

Yes, sir. Shirley was something else. There was only one thing wrong with Shirley: she was too perfect. She was so perfect that I knew she was out of my league. As a matter of fact, I was afraid to speak to her.

I used to lie awake at night dreaming about the beautiful Shirley and thinking what it would be like to be able to say that Shirley was my girl. The insecurities of a teenage boy are not to be taken lightly.

One day toward the end of the seventh grade, our class went on a picnic. We got on the big yellow school bus and went to Grant Park. The beautiful

Shirley was there, and her mere presence made the whole inside of that drab bus fairly glow.

When our teacher announced that we were going to the Cyclorama, a cheer went up that you could hear all the way to Five Points. We got to the Cyclorama about the same time that a busload of retarded children arrived.

They were something to behold. You could see the wonder light up their faces as they saw the Battle of Atlanta. They loved every minute of their tour and asked the teacher countless questions.

All the way back to our picnic area, the beautiful Shirley made fun of those retarded children. She wouldn't quit making snide, cutting remarks and mocking the children.

I got a real education that day at Grant Park. And the beautiful Shirley never looked attractive to me again.

Families tend to pass down the same customs to their children that they learned from their parents. If your mother and father let you open your presents on Christmas Eve rather than Christmas morning, chances are good that you followed that custom with your children.

Well, the same was true with my family; that is, until my youngest daughter, Leigh Ann, came along.

Leigh, one of the most beautiful babies I ever saw, had a mind of her own from the very first. She is four years younger than her brother Phil.

You know, some big brothers can get away with aggravating little sisters just because of the difference in their sizes. Not so with Leigh Ann. She never let Phil get away with anything, and would attack him physically any time he tried to take advantage of her.

I recall one time when he was eight and she was four. He drank her Coca-Cola without asking her. So, without a word, she went upstairs and poured his gold fish out of the second-story window.

She was afraid of *nothing.* Well, almost nothing.

The legend of the Tooth Fairy had always been big at our house, and any time a child lost a tooth he or she could be sure that the Tooth Fairy would take the tooth from under the pillow and leave some money.

When Leigh Ann lost her first tooth, I told her how lucky she was, because she could put her tooth under the pillow, and the Tooth Fairy would come into her room while she was asleep, take the tooth, and leave money.

She started to cry; she said she didn't want the Tooth Hairy in her room while she was asleep, and if that was the only way she could get the money, then the Tooth Hairy could just keep it.

Funny how customs change From that day on, the Tooth Fairy always left the money on top of the TV in the den.

Sex Education for Dick and Jane

It happens every year, the big debate over sex education in the schools. You can set your calendar by the time the debate starts. It's just as dependable as the jonquils coming out or the trees starting to bud.

One side says we must teach sex education to make sure our young folks are prepared to face life and grow up to be strong, emotionally secure adults. The other side says the teachers don't know how to teach it; that there are no college sex education courses for teachers, therefore our teachers are not qualified to pass their knowledge (or lack of it) along to the kiddies.

Oh, how the debate grows! Year after year it seems to grow, with the foolish people on both sides making the most noise.

Just a few short years ago this was all taken care of at home by the parents. The education varied from home to home. In some homes parents taught their offspring they were found in the cabbage patch, while in other homes youngsters were taught that they were delivered by a stork.

Then, as time went on, we became more courageous and started to teach sex education in the schools, but it wasn't called sex education. Oh no.

We weren't ready for that. It was slipped in as part of the health course—worked in somewhere between "personal hygiene" and what kind of vegetables you should eat to be healthy.

How could a subject be this simple and both sides be wrong? It seems to me that the average fellow should be able to figure out the simple fact about teaching sex education in our public schools. It boils down to this: Until they learn to teach about love, about tenderness, about enjoying hearing someone laugh, about the obligations you have to the people you love—until you learn to teach these things, a sex education course is nothing but a course in plumbing.

How Small *Was* It?

Have you ever stopped to think about how much bragging some folks like to do? Now, we tend to look down on folks who brag, but we really shouldn't do that, because we all brag a little. Grandmas brag about their grandchildren, and mamas and daddies love to brag about the exploits of their sons on the Little League field. And oh my! When a daughter becomes a cheerleader, a proud daddy will never let you forget it.

Some folks brag about how rich they are, and some folks brag about how poor they used to be.

Some folks brag about the fact that they have never had a drink, and some folks brag about how much they can drink.

If you want to hear some big-league bragging, just talk to someone who has just lost some weight, or someone who has quit smoking.

Well, it's my turn to brag. I came from a small town, and I want to brag about how small it was. Yes, sir. I come from a *real* small town.

How small was it? I'll tell you how small it was.

It was so small that the cotton gin had an olive in it.

It was so small that the head of the Mafia was Japanese.

My home town was so small that the City Hall had hump-backed mice.

You want to know how small my home town was? Well, it was so small that the local truck stop was a nail.

It was so small that both city limit signs were on the same post.

The biggest church in town was the Fourth Baptist Church.

It was so small that it was forty-five minutes from Atlanta by phone.

Once I was going back there to speak to the Rotary Club, but the guy couldn't get off work.

It used to get real hot in my home town. You wanna know how hot it got in my home town?

Well it got so hot that . . .

Naw, that's a whole 'nother story.

Didn't Hit a Lick

I was ten and my Uncle Harry was about sixteen. He was a real car nut, but I don't guess that's any big deal; most sixteen-year-old boys are car nuts. Harry, however, had done something about it. He had gone to a junkyard and bought an Austin convertible. It was something to behold! We were sure that not another sixteen-year-old in the world had a car that was quite as grand as my Uncle Harry's Austin convertible.

There was only one problem: this darling little car had no top, no motor, and no transmission. Other than that, it was a young boy's dream.

We had more fun planning what we were going to do in it when we got it running than we could have had if it had been a new Cadillac.

I guess we knew deep down that it would never run, but dreaming about it was surely fun. One day we pushed it out on the street next to the curb and were sitting there in it, making plans and day-dreaming, when a man pulled up behind us and hollered out the widow, "You boys need a push?"

There was no hesitation; we answered at the same time, "Yes, sir!"

He put his bumper against ours and down Spring

Street we went. It was great! The wind in our faces and not a care in the world!

We went three blocks and the man got out of his car and said, "Did it ever hit?"

Harry said, "No, sir. It didn't hit a lick."

The man said, "Let's take a right here, and I'll push you over to Ware Avenue and we can get it up to about forty. I betcha it'll crank then!"

We said that would be a good idea, since we knew it was about a mile's free ride. Down Ware Avenue we went, twenty-five, thirty-five, forty-five! It was great!

We came to a stop sign at Semmes Street and the man got out of his car again.

He said, "Wonder why it didn't start?"

And Harry said, "Well, it ain't got no motor."

The man yelled, "No motor! How do you expect it to start with no motor?"

Harry said, "We wasn't expectin' it to start."

The man jumped in his car and burned rubber as he left, screaming cuss words at us till he was out of sight.

Some folks just don't seem to be able to take a joke.

When Mr. Henry Ford figured out how to mass-produce automobiles, he did a fine day's work. Yes, sir, the automobile is one of man's best servants. It just makes everybody's life so much better. When it's running.

Now, if your car is running and doing what it is supposed to do, it's worth whatever you paid for it. But I'm telling you the truth, funseekers; when your car ain't running, it ain't fit to plant flowers in.

I had a car one time that I was so tickled with I could hardly stand it. I bought it brand new, and it had everything you could get on a car. It was even named after an animal. It had the standard warranty, and during the warranty period, it didn't miss a lick. It ran like Niagara Falls.

I was convinced I had the best car in the world.

But the day after the warranty was out, I had to make a trip down to Macon. I was about down to Forsyth, and the sucker quit running. I sat on the road about twenty minutes, cussin' and trying to get it started, and then it started running again. This started a relationship with my car that was to lead to pure hatred on my part. The car would run two or three days and then stop. I had every mechanic in the

Southeast look at it, and they all said the same thing: "Looks all right to me."

In the next six months I put more miles on that car up and down on a grease rack than I did on the road. I finally figured out what the problem was. My car was possessed by a demon.

I called a local psychic and he said he had never removed a demon from a car, but that he had burned one or two for the insurance. I told him I didn't want to do anything dishonest.

Well, about a month later I solved my problem. I traded cars with a Baptist preacher. That was about five years ago, and everytime I see him, I'm shocked. For a preacher, he sure cusses a lot.

Movie producers over the years seem to pull out all the stops to come up with new ways to scare you right out of your Fruit-of-the-Looms. I don't know when it started in Hollywood, but the first monster I can recall from the movies was King Kong. In case you don't remember, King Kong was a very ugly ape with a serious thyroid condition. He was as big as a building and had a temper like a high school principal. And I was convinced that nothing could ever be scarier than old King Kong. But then I saw Frankenstein, a monster as big as an Alabama lineman with an IQ to match.

Many a night's sleep was ruined by nightmares of the Frankenstein Monster.

The years passed, and I thought I had outgrown the scary movies; but then Hollywood got their fright machine into high gear, and Alfred Hitchcock taught us that even a tiny sparrow could scare us while we were in that dark theater.

Then along came *The Exorcist* where a twelve-year-old girl had them climbing the theater walls. And don't forget *Jaws,* where a great white shark became the last word in scary.

Funseekers, if you thought these monsters were scary, I hope you saw the movie on TV the other night. It was called *The Deep,* and the bad guy was an eel. I know what you're thinking: How can a little old eel be scary? Well, let me tell you, this was no ordinary eel. He was big and mean and ugly and had more teeth than the entire Osmond family. Eels are mean, I mean real mean. Did I ever tell you about the eel in Florida that tried to eat a scuba diver? Well, the diver got away and the eel was so hacked off that he waited till the next day, got out of the ocean, caught a Greyhound bus, followed the scuba diver from Daytona Beach to Valdosta and ate him in the Holiday Inn swimming pool.

I don't want you to think I worry about things like eels getting me, but the largest body of water I intend to get into again is going to have a rubber ducky and soap suds in it.

A Lot of Suspicious Characters Stay At San Quentin

My earliest knowledge about prison came from the movies. They called prisons "the big house," or "stir," or "going up the river."

James Cagney or Humphrey Bogart was always the star and played a tough, smart-talking convict. There was always a tough, brutal guard, and he was usually played by Barton McClain or Ward Bond. There was the kindly old guard who played checkers through the bars with the men on death row. The kindly old guard was usually called "Pop."

Every prison movie had a priest. I was thirteen years old before I knew that anyone besides Catholics got the death sentence. The priest was usually played by Pat O'Brien or Alan Hale.

There was always this same black guy on death row. He was standing there holding the bars in movie after movie singing "Swing Low, Sweet Chariot." Great voice, but a very limited repertory.

And Sylvia Sidney was always standing outside the prison on the night of the execution holding onto the bars in the gate and squalling.

This was the view of prison that I had as a child, and it all came from the prison movies. It was just horrible.

In the last few years, it seems to me that the media have taken a very special interest in prisons. Television and newspapers have gone to great lengths to show us that prisons today are just terrible. They are overcrowded, dirty, cold in winter, hot in summer; the food is terrible and the medical care is worse. The guards are brutal, and the place is chock to the brim with very suspicious-looking characters.

Yes, sir. The media have made a great deal of the fact that prisons are not good places to be. That's not a news flash to me; I've known it all my life.

And that's the principal reason, funseekers, that I ain't never been in prison.

Adult Shock

When you were a child, life was so much simpler. It was simple for a lot of reasons. You had no pressure to earn a living, so you could devote most of your time to the better things of life, like playing mumbletypeg or "throw the can" or hide-and-seek.

You could go fishing and take your shoes off and stand in the warm mud. Or you could just lie around and follow the adventures of Captain Marvel, Plasticman, and Wonder Woman in your favorite comic book.

Ah, yeah. Life was so uncomplicated. If you had a question you wanted answered, you just went to a grown-up and you just knew that grown-up had all the answers.

Then one day you looked around and realized that there were no more Captain Marvel comic books and nobody to play hide-and-seek with, and mud just didn't feel the same between your toes.

But the biggest shock to me was that here I was a grown-up and didn't have all the answers. There were so many questions I still had and nobody to answer them, thousands of unanswered questions.

Hey, if you know any of these answers, let me hear from you. For example, why do Hershey bars without almonds cost the same as Hershey bars with almonds? Now, that may not be important to you, but I wonder about it.

And why do gas stations lock the restrooms and leave the cash register open? And if X-rays are harmless, why does the technician hide behind a lead shield? And why do you have to say "aahhh" when the doctor puts that popsicle stick in your mouth? Why can't you say "ooohhh" or "uuuhhh"? Life as a grown-up is so restricting.

Boy, how I would like to find the answers to my questions!

But you know what I would *really* like to find? Just one more time, I would like to find somebody to play hide-and-seek with.

I passed a Little League field the other day and saw about fifty little boys practicing football.

The coaches were busy working. The mamas were sitting in their aluminum chairs.

My mind rushed back fifteen years, to my son Phil's first football practice. He was six years old and knew as much about football as he did about brain surgery.

I had looked forward to that first practice almost since the day he was born. Football had been a great part of my life in high school, and I just knew deep down that Phil was going to be another Jim Thorpe. I had started throwing a football to him as soon as he was big enough to see it coming. We had lots of fun throwing that little plastic football back and forth.

The big day came at last; and if ever there had been a proud daddy, it was me.

Phil was one of the youngest boys on the team, and just did not do well. I cringed as he missed one tackle after another. He was trying; but at that first big practice, he just looked horrible. All the way home in the car, I lectured him about how disappointed I was. He sat beside me and didn't say a word.

We got home; I took him to the back yard, where I intended to make a football player out of him. He still had not spoken. I got him down in a three-point stance, and I got down across from him. I was lecturing, and suddenly I looked up at him. He had one great big tear running down his cheek.

I couldn't believe what I had done. I took him in my arms and sat down in the grass and hugged him.

Here was a fine little boy with the sweetest disposition any child could ever have, and I was upset because of something as trivial as football.

I learned a lesson that I have never forgotten. You see, Phil was a better football player that day than I was a daddy.

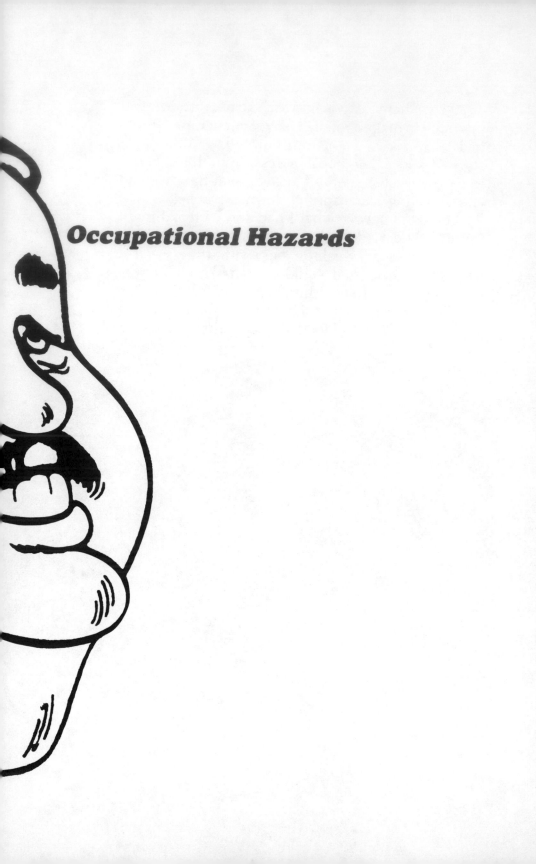

Occupational Hazards

I don't guess a day goes by that somebody doesn't tell me a sure-fire way to lose weight. I wouldn't mind so much, but the people who talk to you about it usually weigh about eighty pounds and have never had a weight problem. Let the record clearly show, funseekers, that I know how to lose weight. I don't know how to keep it off, but I know how to lose it.

In my life I have lost over two thousand pounds. Think about that. Over two thousand pounds. That's the equivalent of a large horse.

I think now you probably understand why I resent some emaciated little runt telling me how to lose weight. Dear Lord, how I detest skinny people! Not only have I tried every diet introduced in this country over the last thirty years, but I have also invented a few that nobody ever heard of. I invented the famous elephant diet. You can have one elephant a week, cooked any way you want it. The only thing is, you have to catch it yourself and kill it with a butter knife.

I guess the wildest thing I ever tried was a hypnotist. A friend of mine knew about a hypnotist named Mandrake Wilson. My friend assured me that

Mandrake could put me under and when I woke up, I'd be all set to give up food.

I decided I'd give Mandrake a try. He was wearing a great velvet turban, a black cape, and no shoes. And, oh yeah! He had a ring on his great toe. I knew one thing right away about Mandrake: he was not from around here.

He laid me down on a rollaway bed, turned the lights down low, put a Lefty Frizell record on, and started to talk to me real soft and slow. Kinda like Clark Gable used to talk to Claudette Colbert. He told me that when he snapped his fingers I would wake up and not be hungry.

He snapped his fingers and I woke up and ate his medallion. It cost me seven-fifty to find out that medallions give me heartburn.

Where's the Service in Service Station?

Whatever happened to the idea that the customer is always right? Now, I know that is a cliché from the past, but a lot of good businesses were built on the customer being right. In case you hadn't noticed it, that's as gone with the wind as Tara is.

Do you remember going into a gas station and the attendant bounding out, smiling and saying, "Can I hep you?" And before you could get out of the service station, he had checked your oil, tires and battery, washed your windshield, and offered to babysit for you on Saturday night.

The first thing you see when you go into a gas station now is a sign that says "due to a shortage of computer parts, the amount shown on the pump represents one-half of your actual purchase." Now, just think about that. There ain't no such thing as a shortage of computer parts. They're just too cheap to buy new pumps, so they let you do their math for them.

The next sign you see is one on the door that says they accept exact amount only. Now think about that for a moment. Exact Amount Only. Now, they want your business, or they wouldn't put their silly commercials on TV. But they only want your

109

business if they don't have to make change or tell you how much the pump says you owe.

Then you go inside to pay. Whatever happened to the smiling attendant? Well, he's still there; he just doesn't go outside any more. Gone forever are the coveralls with his name over the pocket; gone forever is the comment "Looks like you're a quart low." Gone forever is the clean windshield and the checked transmission fluid.

But you know what I think bothers me the most? I feel that it's basically un-American to pay a gas station attendant who has clean hands.

Dr. Kildare Never Wore Bellbottoms

I can stand anything but pain, because I found out years ago that pain hurts. As a matter of fact, the more pain you have, the more it hurts.

The story I'm about to tell you is true; only the names have been changed to prevent a punch in the mouth.

One day I was walking out my back door and tripped and fell down about four steps. I tried to break the fall with my hands out in front of me and really hurt both my wrists. I was in such pain that I was just sure that my chubby little wrists were broken.

I called my doctor's office and his nurse told me that my family doctor was in the hospital. It seems that he had suffered a heart attack while water-skiing. I'll never forgive him for not being available in my hour of need. He's a real nice old boy, but bad to have random heart attacks. I've been telling him for years that he needs to see a good doctor.

Well, to make a long story short—if it isn't too late—I didn't know what to do, so I called a friend and she said she had a great doctor, and she would call him and see if he could see me.

I went to visit this wonderful healer of the wrists. I was really in pain by the time I got to his office.

I told him I was there, and they told me to have a seat in the waiting room. Sitting there, I noticed about four hundred pictures on the walls, all of this doctor, taken in Vietnam. In the pictures he was treating little children and wearing this big .45 automatic on his hip.

Now, when I tell you there were four hundred pictures on the wall, that's no exaggeration. I knew that I was in the office of an egomaniac.

About the time I was getting ready to leave, the receptionist said, "The doctor will see you now."

I was led into a little examining room and told to sit down. I had been there about two minutes when the biggest, ugliest nurse this side of Villa Rica came in with a clipboard and said, "We need to check your weight, Mr. Porch."

I said, "I hope you're just gonna weigh my wrists, because that's all that hurts."

She didn't think it was very funny. She finished weighing me, then she took my temperature, then she checked my blood pressure. Every time she would check something, she would write the results on a clipboard that said ATLANTIC ICE AND COAL on the back of it.

I tell you, funseekers, before that nurse finished with me she had checked everything but my class ring.

As she was leaving the room she said, "The doctor will be with you in a minute."

"Could you get me something for the pain?" I asked. "I'm really hurting."

She said, "You can't have anything till after the doctor sees you. Would you like some water?"

I said, "I'm not dirty, lady. I'm in pain!"

She didn't even smile as she closed the door.

Well, about ten minutes went by, and I was fit to be tied.

Suddenly the great healer came into the room. He had his nurse's clipboard with him. . .you know, the one that said ATLANTIC ICE AND COAL on the back.

I tell you, this doctor was something to behold. He was about five feet tall, and was wearing white bellbottom pants with a flowered Hawaiian shirt and blue tennis shoes.

He came into the room reading his clipboard and never even looked up.

He said, "Mr. Porch, you are fat."

And I said, "Yes, doctor, and you are short. Now, I can leave here and lose weight, but what are you going to do?"

I knew from this moment on that any chance for a good relationship with this doctor was shot to hell. So I left and got myself two Ace bandages and some Bufferin. Then I sacrificed two chickens to the Moon God.

About two years ago, I had to go to New York City on business. Now, New York is a right nice place to visit, but when you are there on business and are in a hurry, the traffic and hustle and bustle can soon get on your nerves.

The folks up there are all in a hurry, and you get the impression that you'd better not interrupt their organized mayhem, because most of them are kind of quarrelsome and would not mind hurting your feelings.

They talk funny, and ain't none of them from around here.

I could feel the hostility as I got off the airplane. I got my luggage and went outside to get a cab. I got in line just in time to see the taxi dispatcher and a customer get in a fist fight about how much the fare should be to Brooklyn. It wasn't a bad fight, but neither one of them could stand a chance against a red-headed south Georgia waitress I know named Roberta.

Well, it finally came my turn and I got in a taxi.

The driver never turned around. I said, "Do you know where 500 Park Avenue is?"

He said, "Jes."

I said, "Sure is a nice day."

He said, "Jes."

I said, "How do you think the Mets will do this year?"

He said, "Jes."

There was a big sign in the taxi that said "Driver will not change any bill larger than $5." The smallest I had was a twenty. I thought, "Here I am nine hundred miles from the nearest glass of buttermilk, stuck in a taxi with the Cisco Kid, and not only can he not change a twenty, but I'm not gonna be able to explain to him that a twenty is the smallest bill I have."

I guess the Lord looks after you when you are north of Richmond, because about that time we came to a toll both. I said, "I'll pay this."

I rolled the window down and handed the toll booth operator my twenty. He made an ugly face and said, "Is that the smallest bill you got, fella?"

I could see the anger in his face. I said, "Jes."

He said, "I hate people who give me big bills."

I said, "Jes."

He took the bill and said something insulting about Puerto Ricans and threw my change in the window.

As we pulled away, I yelled, "How's your mama 'n' 'em?"

If you can't join them, beat them.

I don't particularly like chefs. No, that's not right. It would be more accurate to say that I dislike some chefs. Well, that's not right, either. I guess the fact of the matter is, I hate all chefs.

Now, let me say real quick that I don't dislike cooks. But when cooks stop being cooks and turn into chefs, they become my mortal enemy, because the first thing they do is start to act real stuck-up. They put on a snow-white uniform and a tall silly hat that makes them look like a cross between a polar bear and a Ku Klux Klanner. Then they have to change their names. Leon becomes Heinrich and Bubba becomes Pierre. Then they decide that they know how you should like your steaks.

Now, let me say that I like my steaks well done. It's not that I mind the sight of raw meat, but a well-done steak tastes better to me. Eating a rare steak is to me a lot like chewing Dubble Bubble gum.

I'll never forget the time I was in a real fancy place in Birmingham, Alabama. I told the waiter I wanted my steak well done.

He said, "Chef Ramon is not going to like that."

I said, "Well, Chef Ramon ain't going to eat it, and I'm not either if it ain't well done. And not only

116

that—I don't want nothing on my baked potato but a dob of cow butter."

The waiter walked away muttering something about me being an uncouth barbarian.

Well, you probably guessed the end of the story. My steak came back burned to a crisp. I ate it and didn't say a word.

When the waiter brought my bill, I wrote him a check for the price of the meal, and as I left, I heard the waiter say to the cashier, "Wait 'til he tries to digest that steak."

I turned around and said, "Wait until you try to cash that check."

I'm sure looking forward to the day when microwave ovens make all chefs obsolete.

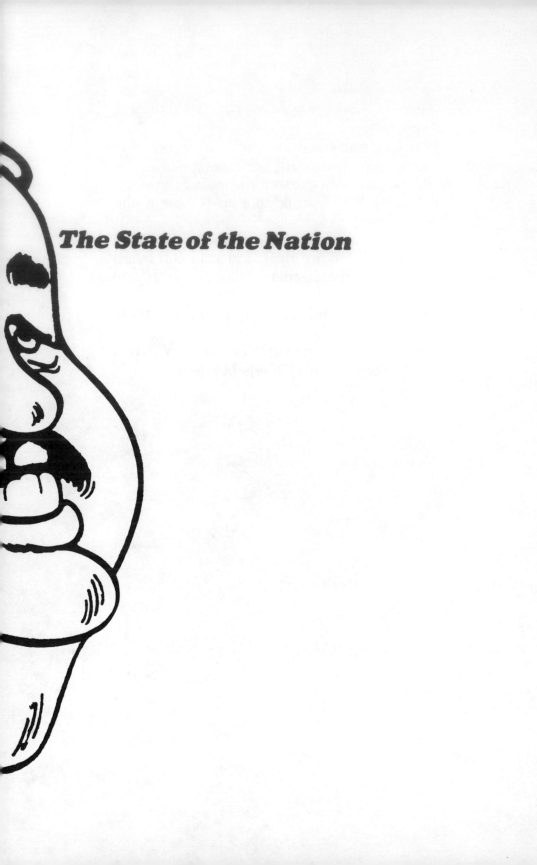

The State of the Nation

An Open Letter to My Favorite Uncle

Dear Uncle Sam,

Well, I know you haven't heard from me in quite some time, so I thought I would drop you a line.

I know you have been just catching fits the last few years, and I just felt like you would like to know that a lot of your nieces and nephews out here still love you. As a matter of fact, Unk, you have always been richly blessed with relatives who not only love you but are willing to go to bat for you anytime you need help.

I guess this family pride started back a couple of hundred years ago, when a relative of yours named Patrick Henry stood up in a Richmond church, shook his fist at his in-laws in Europe, and said, "I know not what course others may take, but as for me, give me liberty or give me death!" And don't forget your nephew Stephen Decatur, who said he was with you, right or wrong.

Oh, yes, Unk. Your folks have always been there, from Bunker Hill to Bella Woods, from Mt. Suribachi to the Chosen Reservoir.

But, Unk, in the last few years some strange things have happened. Folks have pushed you around some, and you have been the soul of patience. Why, they even kidnapped fifty-two of your nieces and nephews. Frankly, Unk, it looks like they have mistaken your goodness for weakness.

Unk, I think it's time you squared away the cockroach countries of the world. Let them know, Unk, we're with you and let them know that anytime, anywhere in the world gangsters and kidnappers want to kick sand in your face, there'll be hell to pay.

Tell them, Unk, that an American embassy is part of this great country, and the next one that is attacked, you're gonna roll up those red-white-and-blue sleeves and make 'em sorry they ever saw the light of day. And Unk, in the name of God, don't let them burn another American flag. No. Not one more.

I guess what I'm trying to say, Unk, is: Do what you have to do to make us proud again, 'cause we're with you and we love you.

Your Nephew,
Ludlow

Meteorology Complicates My Life

I think it was Mark Twain who first said, "Everybody talks about the weather but nobody does anything about it." I guess that's been true since Adam and Eve tried to call Don Hastings to find out how to prune an apple tree.

Any time there is a lull or a dead spot in the conversation, you can count on somebody saying, "Sure is a nice day," or "Mighty cold for this time of the year," or they throw in, "Do you think it's ever going to rain?"

Nope. Still can't do anything about the weather, but boy, how we love to talk about it! Until TV came along, we limited our weather talk to a few of these well-worn phrases, but then one day about the time *I Love Lucy* and *You Bet Your Life* were becoming household words, somebody got the idea that there was a buck to be made doing weather reports on TV. Now, the longer it goes on, the more profitable it becomes and the sillier it gets. Now they make a simple weather forecast a production to rival a Busby Berkeley musical.

The TV moguls decided early on that it wasn't good enough to have weathermen. No, sir, they went out and hired meteorologists. Until Johnny Beckman came along, I thought a high was something you got at cocktail parties.

Have you ever thought of how much trouble TV goes to to tell you that it may rain tomorrow, but it probably won't? They've got satellites floating around in outer space sending us back pictures of the weather. What ever happened to your Uncle Fred's corn that hurt when it was going to rain?

And just plain old regular-issue radar wasn't good enough for them. They had to have Color Radar. I can hardly stand it.

You know what I want to hear just one more time before I die? I want to hear one oldtimer say to another oldtimer, "Looks like a bad cloud acomin' up down Jacks Creek."

And the other old man says, "Yep, when a cloud comes up down Jacks Creek, it's gonna be a frog-strangler."

Stick that in your TV barometer and see who will chart it!

What Good Old Days?

Do you remember just a few short years back, when there were no interstate highways, and when you started to drive from Atlanta to Florida, you knew that you were eight hard hours away from the Florida line? The roads in south Georgia had pot holes that you could lose a Boy Scout troop in. Every barn had "See Rock City" painted on its roof, mules and cows ran loose, and you had to be careful or you'd wind up with a grille full of mule.

Now, it was a hard trip, but I personally feel that it was more fun to travel in those days. The new highways are nice, and nobody is going to argue that they are not safer. But sometimes don't you long for the old days of travel? Take the signs, for example. When was the last time you saw a Burma Shave sign? You sure can't have Burma Shave signs on the interstate, because you drive by so fast, you couldn't tell what the heck they said. Sometimes don't you just yearn to return to the thrilling days of yesteryear when you saw the first little red sign and then watched the jingle unfold? Jingles like:

What you shouted
    May be true
       But did you hear
         What he called you?
           Burma Shave.

Or how about the places where you used to eat? Eating on the road was an adventure in those days. You never knew if you were going to get a gourmet meal or if you were going to be poisoned.

And don't forget the souvenir stores, where you could buy anything from a live baby alligator to a firecracker big enough to blow up Tyler, Texas.

And let's not forget about the south Georgia police officers who protected the natives from the speeding tourist. These folks really enjoyed their work. If they caught you going one mile over the speed limit, they would pull you over and give you their classic line.

They'd walk up to the car and say, "Let me see your drime license."

And then no matter what your license said, or what you said, you got a ticket. But they made it mighty convenient for you; you were allowed to pay your fine right there on the side of the road. Doesn't it make you wonder why we call the good old days "the good old days"?

A recent news story off the wire said that a three-year study in Europe has concluded that fish can feel pain just like animals do. As a result of that finding, Britain's Royal Society for the Prevention of Cruelty to Animals says it may push for outlawing the use of hooks in fishing. Some members of the society argue that the only humane way to catch a fish is with a net.

I don't know for sure if this movement will ever catch on in Great Britain, but I can assure you of one thing: it's almost certain to get some backers in the United States.

Now, the reason I know that is because we just love to pull for the underdog in this country and, after all, who is a bigger underdog than a fish?

You remember the movie, *Jaws*, with that poor old shark being annoyed by all those aggressive swimmers. And do you remember Jonah? He tried his best to choke that whale slap to death.

And then there was Pinocchio. You remember Monstro, that perfectly delightful whale? Well, there he was, swimming around in the ocean, minding his own business, when Pinocchio's daddy sailed that boat right down his throat. Now, I'm gonna tell you the truth: when you swallow a whole sailboat, there ain't enough Rolaids on Earth to help you.

Yes, sir. If you want to see folks get silly, just give 'em a cause to fight for. No more fishing? That's the silliest thing I ever heard of, and if we're going to keep this lunacy from sweeping the country, we've got to band together now.

The first person who walks up to you with an anti-fishing pamphlet, bust him right in the mouth and say something bad about his mama. Fishing and fishermen must be protected at all costs.

I don't know who started this craziness—sounds like the work of a worm.

Circle the Wagons, Boys

We hear stories all the time about how tough life was in the pioneer days, what with Indians, long cold winters and epidemics. But I'm here to tell you, funseekers, that I for one am not emotionally equipped to live in the eighties.

Now, I don't worry about the things that get most of us. I know there ain't nothing I can do about inflation, Afghanistan or ingrown toenails, so I don't worry too much about them, but the little aggravations are enough to make a person crave a persimmon.

It starts every morning when you get in your car and don't buckle your seat belt. It sounds like somebody guttin' a cat, what with the buzzers and lights going off.

I have to tell you, there is a special place in my heart for the old boy who thought of that buzzer, and I firmly believe that everything they say about his mama is true. And how about those safety inspection stickers on your car? If you want to see a policeman come unglued, just let him find one of those stickers with the hole punched in the wrong place.

And another thing. When I was a boy, if you wanted to kill a rat you got you a trap and a piece of cheese, you put it in the back of the cupboard, and by and by you killed yourself a rat. Boy, has all that changed! Now the government gives scientists a bunch of money and they spend it all trying to give that old mouse some kind of disease. Looks to me like the only thing having a rougher time in the eighties than people is the rats. I heard a story about a laboratory rat in Toronto last year. Seems they gave him more diet cola in a week than Orson Welles drinks in a year. On about the sixth day, the rat rolled over on his back, put his darling little feet in the air, belched three times, and shuffled off this mortal coil.

The list of 1980s aggravations just goes on and on—sales tax, income tax, computers, the surgeon general's report, car tags, dog tags, diets, exact change only.

It's enough to make you long for a good old-fashioned Indian attack, isn't it?

Preacher Jackson Brings Home
The Bacon

It seems that about all the news you read in the paper these days is bad. I sometimes just hate to pick up the paper because the news stories all depress me and the editorial page makes me mad; and the sooner Mary Worth starts to mind her own business, the better off we'll all be.

Little Abner and Pogo are both gone, and after twenty years Brenda Starr can't seem to settle down with that one-eyed fellow she married some time back. Have you noticed that Brenda's husband seems to drown a lot?

All in all, the newspapers ain't what they used to be; but every once in a while, there's a story that makes it all worthwhile.

I read one the other day that made me feel good all over.

It seems that there's a preacher out in Pueblo, Colorado, by the name of Oliver Jackson. Now, everybody knows that preachers don't make much money, especially in a town like Pueblo, Colorado, which ain't big enough to have any major-league-type sinning going on.

So in order to save a little money, preacher Jackson got himself a yard full of pigs, sixty-seven in all. Everything was going good 'til the neighbors complained, and the city's animal shelter workers came out and seized all of the Rev's pigs.

Well, there was a great court battle that went on for three weeks. Now, all this time the city's animal shelter was giving them hogs room and board to the tune of $7,400. Well, bless Pat, the city lost the case and the judge ordered the city to pay the tab for keeping and feeding the pigs.

I'm sure the court's decision sounded real legal, but what it boils down to is, never fool with a potential ham hock, 'less you're willing to slop it.

To a Lady Who's Gone

With your permission, I would like to reminisce about a thing that I love very much. I'd like to remember a lady I grew up with who has passed away. I speak of a lady who is gone and can never return. I'm talking about the Atlanta that I grew up with. Now I know what you're saying. You're saying that the new Atlanta is the best Atlanta yet, and I can't disagree with that because I still love her above all cities. But somehow, when you get past forty, you long for things that can be no more. I love the new lady that is called Atlanta. It's a very special place to me, but somehow I can't help feeling a little sad at the death of the old Atlanta.

I remember when a family could ride the trolley to Rich's, get off, and walk to the Paramount Theatre, and it would never occur to them that there was anything to be afraid of.

I remember when the best thing that could happen to a Sunday School class was for the teacher to take them to the old Rollerdrome for a night of roller skating.

I remember when a meal at the Pig and Whistle was the last word in a youngster's catalog of gourmet delights.

131

I remember when we thought the Hurt Building was a skyscraper. And when young boys gave adults their seats on a bus.

I remember when we went to Candler Field, not to catch an airplane, but hoping you would get to see an airplane take off.

I remember when the Southeastern Fair was *the* event of the year.

I remember when we could get a cherry coke at any drugstore in town.

I remember when Bob Montag was the sports hero of every child in Atlanta.

I remember when the Atlanta Crackers would host a three-game series with the Birmingham Barons and sell out old Ponce de Leon Park all three nights.

Yes, sir, the old town's a lot bigger now; but you'd have a hard time convincing me that it's any better.

If You Sing to Me, Sing Country

I have been a country music fan for about as long as I can remember. I was a country music fan long before it was fashionable. I mean I go back to Hank Williams, Roy Acuff, Lefty Frizell, and the immortal Webb Pierce.

What I'm trying to tell you funseekers is this: I was listening to country music when Dolly Parton was still in a training bra. I was listening to country music when Porter Waggoner could only afford one sequin.

I was listening to country music when Merle Haggard was a trusty. I was a country music fan before Danny Thomas became humble.

I mean to tell you, I was a country music fan before Conway Twitty découpaged his hair. What I'm trying to tell you is, I was a country music fan when Oral Roberts was going to a chiropractor.

Got the picture?

Do you know why I'm a country music fan? I'm going to tell you. It's because country music singers don't sing lyrics. Frank Sinatra sings lyrics—Engelbert Humperdinck sings lyrics—Neil Diamond sings lyrics. Country music singers sing words, words that mean something. Words that tug at your heart strings. Words that make you want to cry. Words that make you want to beat up a Commie.

Words that move you; words like "I gotta get drunk and I sure do dread it."

Beautiful, meaningful words like "Our marriage was a failure but our divorce ain't working out either."

Inspiring words like "Drop kick me, Jesus, through the goalposts of Life."

Sad words like "When the phone don't ring, you'll know it's me."

Patriotic words like "Hold my beer, Leon, while I knee Jane Fonda."

Yes, sir, country music is my life. And my life would be complete if somehow, some way, I could get Waylon and Willie to shave.

Poetic License?

Have you ever noticed how many groups there are across the country that have demonstrations? It's hard to listen to a newscast without seeing a group either violently opposed to something or delirious with joy in their support of one cause or another.

Every cause has its supporters, from "Save the Cucumbers" to folks taking up collections to buy Willie Nelson another earring.

I don't want you to misunderstand, though. I believe if folks are upset about something, they ought to let as many people know about it as possible. But there is one thing I don't understand. It seems that I may be the only person in the country who is upset about licenses.

Now I know that some licenses are not only necessary but good. However, we must face the fact that the snowball effect is under way and that licensing is about to get out of hand in this country.

Did you know that in some cities in this great country you must have a license for your bicycle? Think about that for a minute, funseekers. Bicycles today, skateboards tomorrow.

I was talking to a friend of mine the other day who just got back from Florida. He had been down to do some scuba diving, and they wouldn't sell him any air because he didn't have a license. They told him that it was dangerous to scuba dive without a license.

Now, I am not the smartest guy that every lived, but it seems to me that if a fella wants to go out in the ocean and take a chance on drowning or getting hugged to death by an octopus, it ain't nobody's business but his and the octopus's.

So far, they have managed to license guns, cars, dogs, whiskey, barbers, and gambling.

There's just no telling what they'll try to license next. But if I were you, the next time I went into my bedroom, I'd sure remember to lock the door.

Negotiating, Russian Style

I don't know much about the Russians, but I am sure about one thing: they're a nervy crowd. I mean, when they got ready to go into Afghanistan, they just loaded up the troops like they were going to a drive-in movie, rode right up to the border, hung a left, and made themselves right at home. And anybody who tried to stop them got shot.

They didn't try to negotiate, or anything. They just took over.

Am I mistaken, or is a pattern developing? I mean, it seems to me that the Russians only want to negotiate with people that they are not sure they can whip. Look at the record. They didn't want to negotiate with the Hungarian Freedom Fighters, and they sure didn't try to negotiate with the folks in Afghanistan. But boy, how they love to negotiate with Uncle Sam! Did you ever wonder why? Somebody wise once said, "The United States never lost a war or won a conference."

Negotiating with the Russians reminds me of the story about the hunter and the grizzly bear. It seems that the hunter and the grizzly met each other at the watering hole. The hunter raised his rifle and was all set to shoot when the bear spoke.

"Don't shoot," he said. "Let's sit down and negotiate, but first you must put your rifle down."

And they sat down to negotiate. The bear said, "What do you want out of life?"

"A fur coat," the hunter answered. "What do you want out of life?"

"A full belly," the bear said.

In a few minutes the bear got up and left. The hunter was inside a fur coat and the grizzly bear had a full belly. That's negotiation Russian style.

Muggee Conservation

I guess my fondness for westerns goes back to my childhood. I noticed early on that folks from out West had a friendly, easygoing attitude and were just fun folks to be around.

I didn't know it then, but they are real smart, too. Did you know that many of our western states are shooting for zero population growth? They are as big as they want to be, and they know that bigger is not always better.

A concerned citizens' group in New Mexico, in an effort to discourage disillusioned New Yorkers from leaving the Big Apple and moving to the Land of Enchantment, has written a letter to the New York City police commissioner urging him to crack down on the muggers in New York. The letter says, "We in New Mexico are not an unfriendly or unwelcoming breed, but we have all the ex-muggees we can handle. We would like to suggest to your mugging membership that if they don't set up some sort of guidelines, they are going to mug themselves right out of business."

The letter goes on to explain that unless New York City muggers develop some sort of mugging system, all the affluent people will leave the Big Apple, leaving the muggers with no one to mug.

The letter adds, "Then we in New Mexico will be inundated with muggers in search of muggees who blew town."

The group suggests that the police commissioner of New York tell muggers to rotate their victims, and only mug the same person on a quarterly or annual basis, and this way, the victims will not become so discouraged that they will leave New York.

It seems to me that the folks in New Mexico have their finger on the pulse of their state.

New York must crack down and make its muggers practice good old-fashioned conservation. After all, when everybody leaves New York except the muggers, they will have to start mugging each other, and wouldn't that be a shame?

Don't you get sick of the bleeding hearts of the world crying and moaning about gun control? You can't pick up a newspaper without some politician crying about gun control. They say that if you won't register your handguns, then at least, let's have a waiting period of three days before you can take possession of your handgun. Then they say if you won't agree to register your guns and you won't agree to a waiting period, how about crossing your heart and promising not to shoot anybody. Unless of course, they need shooting.

I'm telling you, funseekers, gun control isn't important; as a matter of fact, I think it's a smoke screen that is being put up by the press and big business to hide the real problem that is plaguing this country twenty-four hours a day, 365 days a year.

The problem is a simple one: it's beer bottle control. Do you realize how many skulls are split open nightly by some good old boy swinging a beer bottle?

I'll tell you one thing: it's too many to count. The police don't even keep track

I can just hear the right-wing lobbyist screaming

now. BEER BOTTLES DON'T CUT PEOPLE. ONLY PEOPLE CUT PEOPLE.

Now that the problem is out in the open, I can just see their bumper stickers: "When beer bottles are outlawed, only outlaws will have beer bottles."

Hang your head in shame, Ed McMahon. Tell the people the truth; nobody ever got mean drinking beer out of a .44 magnum.

I know what you military hawks out there are saying:

"If we outlaw beer bottles, we'll be overrun by the Chinese. They're not afraid of atomic bombs, but nobody wants to be cut." Hogwash.

Beer bottles must be registered and registered now.

I know not what course others may take, but I stand with the late Milo Whitlow who said: "Put down that bottle, Sam, or I'll blow a hole in you big enough to play volleyball in."

All Snakes Are Poisonous

Sometimes I think the American public has absolutely lost its mind. Every large city in the country is having financial problems. I don't think anybody would disagree with that. Every large city in the country is trying to save money.

Now, I want you to get the big picture. While firemen, policemen, and school teachers are paid wages that they can't live on, every major city in this country has a zoo with a snake house, where these horrible, ugly creatures are kept in the very lap of luxury. And talk about energy waste! Let me tell you about energy waste. Those snake houses are kept so hot that Lawrence of Arabia couldn't walk through one without fainting.

I know that I'm going to hear from the snake fanciers of the world, singing the praises of everything from King cobras to timber rattlers. But that's all right, because folks that like snakes ain't real bright in the first place.

I have a theory that you can tell a person's intelligence quotient by how afraid he is of snakes.

Smart people don't pick up snakes or fool around with them in any manner. Dummies, on the other hand, like snakes, play with them at every opportunity, and even buy them from pet stores. Their premise is that snakes are nice and that some snakes are not even poisonous. Let me tell you something, fun-seekers. *All snakes are deadly poison.* Even all the little green snakes that spend their time lying around in the grass waiting for someone to come by that they can kill.

Not only that, but snakes are useless. The very most you can hope a snake will do is lie around in his cage and occasionally eat a sweet, cute, defenseless mouse.

I'll tell you what I'd like to see. I'd like to see an enraged citizenry storm every snake house in the country with hoes held high and make snakes as obsolete as Stanley Steamers. They could hang all the snakes, except that the snakes don't have necks.

I think my Uncle Renfro summed it all up when he said, "You can't can't trust anything that ain't got eyelids."

Unforgettable– And Forgettable– Characters

The Schnozz Is Gone

I guess we all knew it was coming. After all, he had been sick since 1972, and he was eighty-six years old. But when I heard the news, it just didn't seem possible. Jimmy Durante—dead.

I guess everybody in the public eye has people who love them and people who hate them. But I don't recall anyone saying anything bad about The Schnozz.

In his long, productive life, he earned a fortune and gave most of it away to good causes.

Durante left school in the seventh grade, never to return. His ambition was a simple one: to earn a living playing the piano. By the time he was seventeen, he was playing old-time piano in a Coney Island bar.

In 1923 he formed a vaudeville act with Lou Clayton and Eddie Jackson. They were featured on Broadway and in vaudeville houses all over the country, and they were known as Clayton, Jackson and Durante. Durante soon emerged as the star of the act with his ad libs at the piano.

He made his first movie in 1931 and became a national favorite almost at once. In the years that followed, he conquered every medium of show business—nightclubs, burlesque, vaudeville, the

Broadway theater, radio, motion pictures, and finally television.

Jimmy Durante, dead at eighty-six. It is still hard to imagine. I guess it's so hard to accept because those of us who loved him know that he will never die as long as there is one of us around who remembers how he would gravel-voice his way through Inka-Dinka-Do, and how he would suddenly jump up from the piano, shouting "Stop the music! Stop the music!" or how he would fracture the language. Remember how catastrophe became "catastastrof" when Durante got excited? He was fond of saying, "Love me, love my nose!"

Well, Mr. Durante. We did love you and we did love your nose. And right now, I just hope that you and Mrs. Calabash are having your long-awaited reunion.

"The Man Just Whipped Me"

It was a boxing fan's delight the other night on television. They televised four championship bouts in one night. It was great, but as I watched the interview I was struck with the thought: whatever happened to the modest athlete?

My mind rushed back to some of the great champions of the past, the interviews they had given and the public statements they had made.

I thought about Joe Louis. After Joe's first defeat at the hands of the German heavyweight Max Schmeling, Joe said, "The man just whipped me." No excuses. No screaming about life's injustices. Just a simple statement: "The man just whipped me." When Joe was asked about his poor showing against Auturo Godoy, Joe said, "I was stale. I couldn't do nothing."

On October 26, 1951, an aging Brown Bomber got into the ring with the young, tough Rocky Marciano. It was the classic mismatch; Rocky was destined to become the heavyweight champ, and Louis was long since over the hill. It was just a matter of time from the first bell. Gone was the blazing speed that made Louis the greatest champ in history. Gone was the beautiful left jab that had been so quick it photographed in a blur. The only thing that you recognized of the old Louis was his great fighting heart.

Finally, Marciano connected, and Joe fell face-down. It was over. Marciano said in an interview, "Joe didn't know he was my hero when I was growing up in Brockton, Massachusetts. The writers said I flattened him and turned my back. They didn't know I was crying." Those were the words of a great champ and, what's more important, the words of a great gentleman.

I know that our current crop of champions is a fine group of men and women and probably the best athletes in history, but quiet, sure modesty does not seem to be one of its long suits.

In the Fifties, We Called It Crazy

I guess if Jake was a teenager today folks would say that he had some sort of emotional problem. But since he was a teenager in the fifties, we all agreed that he was crazy. Now, I don't mean crazy like insane, I mean crazy like strange—crazy like wild.

Let me tell you what I mean. One day Jake and I went to a movie.

I said, "Let's sit over there," and started toward the right side of the theater.

He said, "I can't sit over there."

"Why not?" I asked.

"Because I'm left-handed," he answered.

Got the picture? Old Jake was about a half bubble out of plumb. He used to drive his daddy's car down Main Street so fast that finally the chief of police told him that if he ever caught him walking down Main Street, he was going to put him in jail, and if by chance he caught Jake driving a car again, he was going to ask for the death penalty.

But Jake was not a person to be intimidated by idle threats, because from that day on, Jake dedicated his life to running the police chief as crazy as he was.

Jake did strange and awful things like shaving a billy goat and turning it loose in the middle of Miss Emma Renfroe's pre-baptismal brunch. I remember the time he went to the cemetery the night before poor old Mr. Callahan's funeral and filled the grave back up with dirt. When the folks got there that afternoon to bury Mr. Callahan, there was no place to put the poor old soul.

And Jake had a strange sense of humor. I'll never forget the time he welded a piece of piano wire over the basketball hoops at the gym. It took almost a full scoreless quarter before they found out what was going on.

The last thing I heard about Jake was a little story in the paper that said he had been arrested for running naked across the Agnes Scott College campus. I really thought it was nice when I read later that the students at Agnes Scott held a "Free Jake" rally and raised enough money for his bail. He was strange, but he apparently made a pretty good impression on the Agnes Scott students.

151

Roy Rogers Is a Tacky Person

I never had the chance to meet Trigger; as a matter of fact, I never even met Roy Rogers. The only thing I know for sure about Trigger, outside the movies, is that when he died Roy had him stuffed and put in his museum. That may be the tackiest thing I've heard of since our preacher showed up barefoot at the quarterly meeting. But all in all, I guess a man has a right to do what he wants to with his dead horse.

Trigger was a fine-looking horse, and when Roy put that silver saddle on him, he was a sight to behold. And smart, too. If we can believe the movies, that horse was a lot smarter than Gabby Hayes and the Sons of the Pioneers put together.

I've been around horses most of my life, and they didn't show in the movies a lot about old Trigger. For example, they never showed Trigger stepping on Roy's foot. They didn't even show him biting a plug out of some poor fool who turned his back for a moment. They never did show you how old Trigger would turn over his water bucket or blow all the air out of his lungs while Roy was trying to cinch him up.

They would show Roy riding Trigger about seventy-five miles an hour, but they never did show

Trigger trying to scrape Roy off against a tree.

They showed Trigger going down into the mine shaft to bite through the ropes tied to Roy's hands while the fuse on the dynamite was burning. But they never showed Trigger throwing Roy for a flip because Trigger shied at a feed sack in the trail.

Yeah, you just got to admit that Trigger has some good PR.

I read the other day that when Bullet, Roy's German shepherd, died, Roy had him stuffed, and there they are, Trigger and Bullet, stuffed and standing side by side in that museum. Kinda makes you hope Dale will outlive Roy, doesn't it?

Hi Ho, Silver!

Anyone who knows about horses would agree with two things: one, a horse is one of God's most beautiful creatures, and two, it is one of the dumbest.

Most people get their knowledge about horses from the movies, but I'm here to tell you, funseekers, My Friend Flicka ain't got the brains of a hammer handle. What else besides a horse would go over the same bridge day after day with no problem, and then suddenly panic when it notices the bridge has been painted?

What else besides a horse would be terrified by its own image in a pool of water?

What else besides a horse would not only bite the hand that feeds it, but on occasion try to kick its benefactor's brains out?

I have owned horses on and off for most of my life, and I enjoy everything about them, but they can be more trouble than a pocketful of bumblebees.

I once had a beautiful horse named Silver. I named him Silver because he was white. (Well, it would have been silly to name him White.) Anyway, this was a beautiful horse, but not only was he dumb, he was also mean.

One day my son was riding him and tried to get him to cross a stream. Silver was afraid to go into the water, but after some prompting, he started to cross.

Well, bless Pat! He liked the water so well he decided to take a bath, and he lay down and started to roll over and over with rider, saddle, and all getting soaked and almost drowning.

Silver would bite and kick and stomp. I guess the only thing he didn't try to hurt me with was a switchblade knife.

I finally decided that it was him or me, and if I didn't get rid of him, he was going to kill me. So I traded him off to an old boy for a cypress fence post.

You know, it just didn't seem fair; the Lone Ranger had a horse named Silver, but that was different. The Lone Ranger kept hollering "Hi ho, Silver!" But all I ever hollered was "Oh, hell, Silver!"

Not All Man's Best Friends Are Dogs

Malcolm was probably one of the best friends I ever had. Well, I guess I'd better qualify that, because although I was a great admirer of his, Malcolm didn't really like me. As a matter of fact, Malcolm didn't like anybody or anything.

You see, Malcolm was a big ugly tomcat that I owned when I was a little boy. Now, to say I owned Malcolm would not be a true statement. The fact of the matter is, we lived in the same house, but it was never clear who owned whom.

Malcolm did not know about being afraid. He still holds several records for MEAN. In one twenty-four-hour period, he treed a poodle and a garbage man and totaled out a 1951 Henry J automobile.

Malcolm had little things he liked to do. He would flatten himself out on a mimosa limb, and when Mr. Johnson, our mailman, would pass, Malcolm would drop down on Mr. Johnson's back, scratching and biting and hissing like he was going to kill him. Well, poor old Mr. Johnson would do the only smart thing; he would drop his mail bag and leave the area.

You should have seen old Malcolm burying that mail. He must have run the postal inspectors about crazy.

One day Malcolm followed me to school, and before I knew it, there he was, under my desk. I was in the fifth grade, and my teacher was Miss Watkins. When Miss Watkins saw old Malcolm, she told me to pick him up and take him out of the class. I told her I sure would like to do that, but Malcolm didn't like to be picked up, and if I tried, I was afraid he would gut me like a chicken. I tried to explain to her that Malcolm was not a tolerant cat.

Well, nothing would do her but to get old Malcolm out of that classroom. So she called for James, the custodian. (He was really a janitor, but they could get away with paying him less if they called him something like "custodian.")

James came and said, "I'll get rid of that old tomcat."

Now, picking Malcolm up was not too hard, but putting him down could be real, real tough. Well, when the plaster had quit falling, James' coveralls looked like he had spent the night in a wide-open Mixmaster, the class was a wreck, and they had to turn school out for the day.

I told you Malcolm was the best friend I ever had.

Some Boys Will Be . . .

People love to say, "Boys will be boys." The folks who say that the most are people who just found out that their teenage son just did something awful. If you remember your teen years, it won't take you long to name the boys who were always in trouble.

I have never really been satisfied in my own mind whether these boys were really bad, or if they were just creative. Let me explain that. It took no imagination just to be mean or to play hookey, and you soon forgot those boys' names and their crimes. But there were always one or two who were so creative in their devilment that you never forgot them.

Take, for example, Gascap Bates. His real name was Warren Bates, but we called him Gascap because one time he ran his car into a semi and all that was left of the car was the gas cap.

Old Gascap was a car nut, and all of his meanness seemed to revolve around his car.

One Saturday night the girls' basketball team had a spend-the-night party at Martha Wilson's house, and about eight o'clock Sunday morning, Gascap showed up there in his car. When Sara Ann saw Gascap drive up, she decided it would be cute to run outside in her granny gown and have some fun with old Gascap. It was not a very revealing gown, and she did not think it would be immodest to go outside in, so out the front door she bounded and jumped on the running board of Gascap's car. She stuck her head in the window and said "Take me to ride, Gascap."

That was a mistake, and Sara Ann knew it as soon as Gascap rolled the window up on her neck and started to burn rubber out of the driveway. Sara Ann was screaming, "Stop the car! Stop the car!" but Gascap laughed like a crazy man.

Well, he drove her all over town at about fifty miles an hour, and Sara Ann couldn't figure out what to do with her hands—hold on and keep from being killed or hold her gown down and keep from being embarrassed.

I won't tell you what she decided, but from that day on, the whole town felt like they knew Sara Ann a little better.

Lowell Was a Whino

Do you know any hypochondriacs? There are all kinds, and some are so bad about it that it controls their lives. Once they are convinced that they've got some disease, no doctor on earth can convince them otherwise.

Well, I have a friend named Lowell, and over the last twenty years, Lowell has been convinced that he had every known malady from the bubonic plague to the mange.

I'd call Lowell on the phone and say, "Hey, buddy! Let's go fishing!" And he'd start to whine and say, "I can't go out in this weather. You know about my sinus condition. If I even get my feet wet, it could go into pneumonia, and I probably wouldn't last the night. And you know that my malaria acts up in this kind of weather."

Now, I'm a sympathetic person by nature, but after putting up with this for twenty years, it just got hard to take. So I decided to cure Lowell of his hypochondria.

We were having lunch in a real nice French restaurant and Lowell said, "You know, I feel better today than I have in a long time." He said, "As a matter of fact, I feel perfect, except for a little pain in my shoulder. Nothing serious, just a little twinge."

I said, "That's a shame, but there's a lot of that going around."

He said, "A lot of what going around?"

"Oh, haven't you heard?" I said. "There's a shoulder cancer epidemic in the Atlanta area."

"Oh, my God," he said. "I've got it! How does it affect you?"

"It doesn't affect you at all," I said. "You just die."

Lowell stood up in the middle of the restaurant and screamed, "Dear Lord! I'm dying! I'm dying!"

With that he ran out the front door screaming for a priest. I thought that was kind of strange, since Lowell has been a lifelong Methodist.

I haven't seen Lowell in about two months. The last time we talked, he said he thought he had heartworms and had an appointment with a vet on the following Tuesday.

Malcolm and Herschel

I've told you about Malcolm before. Malcolm was my big ugly tomcat. Not only was he big and ugly, but he was mean. To the best of my knowledge, Malcolm was the only tomcat that ever chased a German shepherd up a tree.

It's hard to put into words exactly how mean he was, but let me say this: There was nothing on the face of the earth that walked, crawled, wiggled, or flew that Malcolm wouldn't fight.

One time my friend Gerry called me and said he and his family were going on vacation. He asked if I could take care of his parrot Herschel while he was gone. I was about thirteen, and it sounded like great fun to be able to look after a genuine talking parrot for two weeks. I cleared it with my mother, and Gerry brought Herschel over, along with his food and a great big cage.

Before he left, Gerry told me that Herschel really hated cats and could take that big hooked bill and do great bodily harm to any cat he could get to. I agreed that I would keep him in his cage and away from Malcolm at all costs; while I felt like my cat could look after himself, I did not want to take any chances of his losing an ear to that razor-sharp bill of Herschel's.

Everything went fine until Herschel got bored and decided to have some fun at Malcolm's expense. He started to holler real loud, "Here kitty, kitty. Here kitty, kitty—time to eat—come get some food."

Now Malcolm, who was always ready to eat, went right to the cage that we had hanging from a hook in the ceiling.

He was trying to figure out who was calling him to eat when that parrot dumped his drinking water in Malcolm's face. In one bound, Malcolm was on the cage. He tore the door off, and he and Herschel had at it. By the time we got into the room, Herschel was gone and Malcolm was standing in the cage growling.

It took us three days to discover that Herschel was hiding in the bread box, eyes glassy, repeating over and over, "Nice kitty, nice kitty."

Funny thing, that parrot's feathers never did grow back.

Cousin Doodle Is a Great American

Did I ever tell you about my Cousin Doodle? Cousin Doodle is a Great American. He is a stock car racer, and he can drive a stock car better than Dolly Parton can float. But that's not the reason he's a Great American.

Cousin Doodle likes to drink beer. He can drink more beer in one day than Laverne and Shirley can bottle in a week. But that's not the reason he is a Great American.

Cousin Doodle is a Waylon Jennings fan. Well, that's somewhat of an understatement. To say he's a Waylon Jennings fan is like saying Columbus used to go sailing.

Doodle would rather hear Waylon sing one song than be in a woman's prison with a handful of pardons.

But that's not the reason he's a Great American.

Doodle is a Great American because he knows how to handle himself in any situation.

One time I was driving him home and my car started to skip. Doodle said to drive eighty and it would quit skipping.

"Are you sure?" I asked.

He said, "Are grits groceries?"

I figured he knew, so I drove eighty. The policeman who caught me drove eighty-five. He pulled me over and stopped his car behind mine.

"Let me handle this," Doodle said. "Do exactly as I tell you. Lock your door, roll up the window, and look straight ahead. Don't look at the policeman, no matter what he says or does."

I told you Doodle can handle any situation, so I did exactly what he said.

The policeman walked up to my side of the car and growled, "Where do you think you are, fat boy? Indianapolis?"

I looked straight ahead and didn't move a muscle. Doodle motioned the policeman to come around to his side of the car, where he had rolled his window down.

The policeman went around to Doodle's side and barked, "Let me see your driver's license!"

Doodle said, "Go to hell! I wasn't driving."

Well, the upshot of the whole thing was that Doodle offered the policeman a four-dollar bribe, and he put us both in jail.

Now, I want to remember that I said Cousin Doodle was a Great American. I never said he was smart.

Junebug

When you look back on your childhood, you kinda wonder how you ever survived. I
mean, we all did such crazy, unthinking things, from
driving too fast to playing with firecrackers; it's really
kind of scary.

I can assure you of one thing: if our children ever
pulled some of the shenanigans we did, we'd be fit to
be tied.

Take my friend, Junebug. He was a great fellow,
but he didn't have the brains of a shotgun shell.

He would do wild, strange things. As a matter of
fact, he would do almost anything to get attention.

He was the first person I ever knew to streak, only
in those days they didn't call it streaking: they called
it "running naked."

Junebug took running naked to new heights. I'll
never forget the time he got the idea that he wanted
to eat some of those little finger sandwiches that Mrs.
Rollins always served in the basement of the church
at her Ladies' Garden Club meeting.

Junebug knew that he couldn't just walk in there
and tell those ladies that he sure would admire having
one of those dandy little finger sandwiches. He was
afraid it would get back to his mama, and she'd wear
him out till his pants wouldn't hold shucks.

So he figured out a plan. He went home and got his cow Priscilla. He took that old cow to the back door of the church. Then he took off his clothes till he was as naked as a pound of sausage, and he rode that cow in the back door just about the time the ladies were in the middle of the pledge to the flag.

Well, funseekers, the ladies went out of both doors and through one stained-glass window, and old Junebug suddenly fell heir to about fifty of those little finger sandwiches.

There's only one thing about this that I don't understand. When the police investigated this occurrence, none of the ladies was able to identify Junebug, and three of them hadn't noticed that he was riding a cow. That always struck me as strange.

On the Trail of Maynelle

If you don't read the personal column of your local newspaper, you are missing some of the best drama since Ma Perkins went off the air.

I was reading the personal column of February 10. The one that caught my eye read:

"Maynelle, you know I love you more than life, and I would do anything on Earth for you. I would climb the highest mountain or wade through the slimiest swamp just to stand by your side and bask in the radiance of your beauty. However, if you don't come back and bring my money and Phillips 66 credit card that you stole out of my pants while I was asleep at the Dixie Motel just outside Waycross, I'm going to track you down and beat both your eyes closed." It was signed Eugene Lamar.

Now, I thought that was kind of touching. Then on February 16 there was more to the story. The personal column said:

"Dear Eugene Lamar: The last time I saw Maynelle, she was getting on a Greyhound bus in College Park. She had a new hairdo with blond streaks and she was dressed up like a million dollars. She had some of them expensive orange

Samsonite suitcases with her. I couldn't believe that she would leave me without even a word. Ben Hadd."

I was really getting hooked on this story, because on March 1, the personal column said:

"Dear Eugene Lamar and Ben Hadd. I saw Maynelle last Tuesday dancing on the table and eating raw wieners at Sam's Place just outside Carrollton, Georgia. When she left town she took my stereo and my collection of Tennessee Ernie's Favorite Gospel Hits. Looks like she's headed West, boys. Lonely in Carrollton."

Well, about a month later I saw a Birmingham, Alabama, newspaper story that said:

"On Saturday, April 3, Maynelle Wiggins became the bride of Spencer J. Rutledge. The bride is from Waycross, Georgia, and the groom is the president of the Last National Bank. The couple will honeymoon in Paris and make their home in the south of France."

I never met the lovely Maynelle, but I bet you one thing: I'll bet she's a good old girl.

Junebug was a real misfit. He was about fifteen years old and couldn't do anything right. He was about two years older than the rest of us; he had failed a couple of years of school. He didn't like to play baseball and the rest of us did; he didn't like to ride Flexiracers and the rest of us did.

Looking back on it, I realize it was kind of pitiful—Junebug wanted to fit in so bad, but he just didn't fit. He felt like if he could do something that nobody else would do, then maybe he could gain some acceptance. But nothing seemed to help.

Well, one day we were all down at the wash hole. In case you don't know what a wash hole is, it is a dammed-up creek. We used to swim in our wash hole. There was a pine tree on the edge of the wash hole, and we were all sitting around one day when somebody said, "Wouldn't it be something if you could dive out of that pine tree into the water?"

We decided that it was impossible since the place you would hit the water was only about two feet deep. We had decided it was too dangerous when old Junebug said, "I can do it!"

We said, "Naw, it's too dangerous."

But Junebug was up that tree in a flash. He stood on a limb, gave a Tarzan yell, and came out

170

head-first. He hit the water and went slap to his shoulders in the mud and the sand.

We pulled him up on the bank and he was out cold. I thought for a minute he was dead, but he finally came around. We laughed and slapped him on the back and told him he had more nerve than an abscessed tooth. About that time Jake Mullins came walking up. We told him what had happened.

Old Jake said, "Can't nobody do that."

Junebug said, "Wanna see me do it again?"

And up the tree he went. Another Tarzan yell and here he came, elbows and knees flailing.

Blop! Right into the two feet of water, mud and sand. We pulled him out again, half conscious.

I guess Junebug made that dive about twenty-five times before the summer was over. I know we should have learned something about courage, but we didn't. I do feel, though, that we learned a lot about Dumb.

Meanness Doesn't Amount to What It Used To

I think there is a trend in this country that I, for one, regard as healthy. Have you ever noticed that people don't seem to be as mean as they used to be? Now, you can say what you want to about violence on TV and the movies, but I for one think Americans are mellowing. When is the last time you ran across a real mean person? I don't mean someone who is just irritable or quarrelsome, I mean someone who regards meanness as a status symbol and everything he does or says is mean—someone like Luke Whitlock.

Now, Luke worked at Mindanaurs Body Shop when he wasn't in jail. And meanness was a way of life with him. He was so mean that he didn't have tattoos; he had iron-on transfers. His proudest possession was a T-shirt that said "I hate earthlings."

He had two things that he did for relaxation. He would stop at the Methodist Church on Sunday morning and somewhere between "How Great Thou Art" and "Amazing Grace," he would attack the choir with a chair. And if that didn't entertain him sufficiently, he would go out in the parking lot and rip the bumpers off the cars.

Unfortunately, Luke is no longer with us. He passed away in 1978. It was really tragic. It all happened at the Chateau Switchblade, which was Luke's favorite beer joint.

Buzz Jackson bet Luke five dollars that he couldn't drink a gallon of gasoline. Luke took the bet, but only on the condition that it be Amoco unleaded, because that was the only kind that didn't give him heartburn.

It was a sight to behold: old Luke sitting at the bar with a gallon fruit jar of Amoco unleaded in front of him, the crowd gathered around singing, "Save a gallon, save a gallon of gas a week."

Now this next part may be hard to believe, but it's the gospel truth. Luke chugalugged that Amoco unleaded and then chased it with a can of 10W40 to kind of settle his stomach. Everything was going fine till Luke decided to light a cigarette. He no more than had his Zippo flaming when he inhaled and his belly button blew out. He died instantly.

Yes, sir. Old Luke was something else. There may never be another like him, and that will make the world a better place.

I went to see a great movie the other night; it's called *The Great Santini*. If you get a chance, catch it; you won't be disappointed.

I was trying to figure out later why I enjoyed it so much, and it finally came to me. It's a movie that could have been made in the thirties or forties. Just good old-fashioned entertainment, where you laugh a lot and cry some.

They're making a few good movies now, but nothing like they used to.

I went to see a cowboy movie not long ago, and not only was the language foul and the action bloody, but it had more sex in it than a Friday night in Tijuana.

Now I don't know anything about making movies, but I know what a cowboy picture is supposed to have in it; and what's more important, I know what's not supposed to be in it.

First of all, the blood is unnecessary. Now I guess I must have seen ten or twenty thousand cowboy movies starring folks like Roy Rogers, Gene Autry, Hopalong Cassidy, and Bob Steele.

I don't recall ever seeing anybody bleeding. Oh, maybe a little bit out of the corner of their mouth, after a fist fight—but that was it.

They didn't need all the blood and gore—you knew that if Bob Steele knocked a man off a five-hundred-foot cliff, the sucker was dead. And when Rod Cameron shot a man and he fell down, you could bet your buckskins on two things: number one, he was dead; and number two, he needed killing.

Now let's talk about sex. Can you imagine seeing Lash LaRue in bed with a woman? Not only did Lash never take off his hat, but just think what those spurs would do to a Beautyrest mattress. That's the reason cowboys always slept outdoors on the ground. Spurs are murder on bed linens.

As for all the cussing, what does that prove? I guess the worst language I heard in a movie as a child was Gabby Hayes saying "Goldarn it." And even when John Wayne swore vengeance, he did it without cussing. And if you know anything about John Wayne, you know that when he swore vengeance, he swore vengeance with a vengeance.

Say what you want to about realism, I'll take fantasy every time.

Harry

Harry was my uncle, but since he was only six years older than I, he was much more like a brother than an uncle.

My father died in 1936 when I was twenty-one months old. My mother, who was just past twenty, had no choice but to take me and return to her mother and father. I was fortunate to be reared in that beautiful, loving home.

Harry was my mother's baby brother and he soon became my big brother. Harry and I never got along as children. As a matter of fact, my memory seems to evolve around a twenty-year fist fight between me and Harry.

Like most big brothers, Harry pretty much regarded me as a pest, and I was fair game for any prank he could think up. I'll never forget the time I had the mumps. I felt pretty good, but my grandmother had told me it was important not only that I stay in bed, but that I stay very still in bed. It was explained to me that if I was not real still, the mumps would "go down" on me. I asked what that meant, and my grandmother said it was too complicated to explain, but if the mumps went down I could never be a daddy. Well, it worked, because it

176

turned me into a very good patient. I was afraid to move my eyes.

One day while I was out of school with the mumps, I was left at home alone. My grandmother said, "Don't worry. Harry will be home in about fifteen minutes and he will look after you while I'm shopping."

I was left alone, and sure enough, my red-headed Uncle Harry showed up in about fifteen minutes.

The first thing Harry did was to jump right in the middle of the bed and start to use it like a trampoline. I was bouncing halfway to the ceiling, screaming "Stop! Stop! The mumps'll go down on me!"

Harry kept bouncing, laughing like a loon at the horror I was showing about my manhood. You see, Harry had one single rule in his dealing with me: it was okay for him to beat me silly anytime he felt like it.

It was okay for him to treat me like a dog or scare me to death with tales of the Wolfman or the Frankenstein monster, but if anyone else ever touched me, it was hell to pay, because they had to fight Harry.

I don't understand to this day the logic behind his thinking. He could put my lights out whenever he pleased, but when the chips were down and I really needed him, he was always there. And I mean *always*.

The fist fights continued, and as I got older I was able to win once in a while. The hostility turned to respect as I could hold my own in a fight, and then gradually the respect turned to a deep and warm brotherly love.

177

During the last days of World War II, Harry joined the army. For the first time in my life, Harry was not there. I didn't know it was possible to miss another human being so much.

I didn't know it then, but my life would never be the same again. We were growing up and therefore growing apart.

Harry came back from the army and got married. We saw each other a lot, and he was still my big brother. The years passed and I went into the Marines, came home, went to law school, and had a family of my own. Harry was thirty-six and I was thirty. We were both in the insurance business and we would sometimes get together and talk shop.

Late one night my phone rang and woke me out of a sound sleep. It was my Aunt Edna. She said Harry had been in a bad accident and he was at the Georgia Baptist Hospital.

"Please hurry," she said. "Please, please *hurry*!"

I was in my car in less than five minutes and at the emergency room in less than twenty minutes. I stopped the first nurse I could find.

"Where is Harry Kidd?" I asked.

"Oh, he was DOA," she said matter-of-factly.

I knew there was a mistake. Harry couldn't be dead. That wasn't possible. I got into my car and drove to where Harry lived. The house was crowded and I knew that it was true. I had to get inside and talk to Shirley, Harry's wife. Shirley would need me.

The living room was full of well-meaning friends. I put my arms around Shirley, and she said, "Don't give me a shoulder to cry on."

My God! It was true; Harrry was dead. My big brother was dead!

I was numb. It seemed to hit me all at once, and I slumped into a chair. Nearby two men were talking.

"How did he do it?" one man asked.

The other man said, "He ran a hose from the exhaust pipe into the car. Did he leave a note?"

I walked out and got into my car and drove as far as I could. Then I pulled off to the side of the road and cried for fifteen minutes. I had never felt so alone before or since.

I used to visit his grave a lot, but never went there without crying. I'm not an overly religious person, but I am sure of one thing: when I finally make that walk to those old pearly gates, my big brother will be right there to show me the ropes.

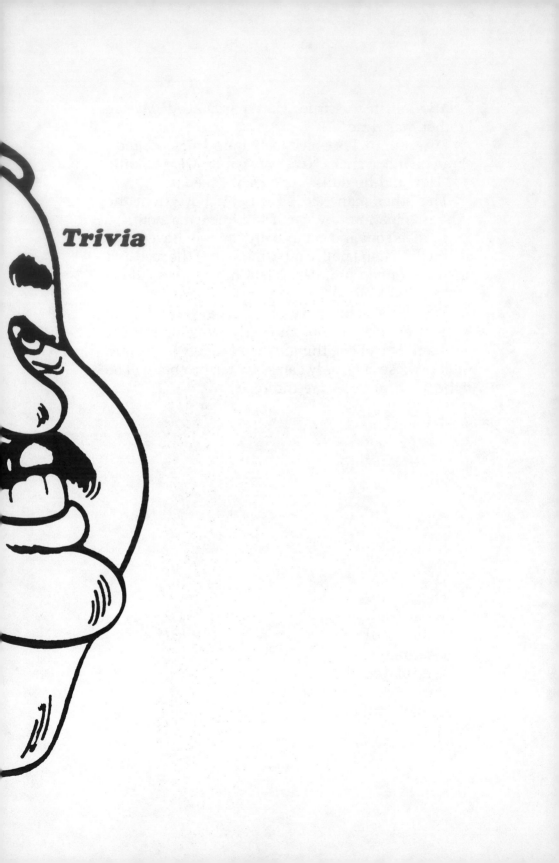

Trivia

Trivia

When my friends found out that I was writing a book they all said the same thing, "What's the book about? Trivia?"

Therefore, I felt that a chapter on trivia was a must. I have played trivia all over the country; I have played trivia on forty or fifty radio stations and on the Mike Douglas television show. The more trivia I play the more friends I make, and that's the principal benefit of my favorite game.

You will note that I don't have any trivia answers in the book. Only questions. If you have trouble with any answers, come see me.

1. What two men played *The Great Gildersleeve?*
2. Who played Will Stockdale on TV?
3. Who was the voice of TV's "My Mother, the Car"?
4. On TV's "O. Henry Playhouse," who played O. Henry?
5. What was Doc Blanchard's real first name?
6. Who was the first woman to swim the English Channel?
7. Who played Alvin York's two drunken buddies in the movie classic, *Sergeant York?*
8. Name the Lone Ranger's nephew.

9. What was Van Johnson's name in *Battle-ground*?
10. Who was the voice of Jiminy Cricket in Walt Disney's *Pinocchio*?
11. Who played the Wizard in *The Wizard of Oz*?
12. Who was the voice on *The March of Time*?
13. Who made "Donkey Serenade" famous?
14. Who was John Agar's wife in *Sands of Iwo Jima*?
15. Who was Alice Lon?
16. Who was Johnny Roventinni?
17. Who wrote *The Legend of Sleepy Hollow*?
18. In *Blondie*, what is Mr. Dithers' first name?
19. Name five movies in which John Wayne died.
20. What was the name of the boat on "Gilligan's Island"?
21. Who played Jim Bowie on TV?
22. Wally Cox had a TV show after "Mr. Peepers." Name it.
23. What was the name of Herb Schreiner's TV show?
24. What did W.C. Fields do before he became a comedian?
25. Who was Harry Lime?
26. Who was Percy Dove Tonsils?
27. What is Daisy Mae's maiden name?
28. Who killed John Wilkes Booth?
29. Name the owner of the boarding house on "Gunsmoke."
30. Who was the youngest man ever to become a heavyweight champion?
31. What was Fibber McGee and Molly's home address?

32. Who was the Yankee soldier who was killed by Scarlett O'Hara in *Gone With the Wind*?
33. Who played the Mexican bandit in *Treasure of Sierra Madre*?
34. Who played the singing candy salesman in *Rose of Washington Square*?
35. How long was the Camptown Racetrack?
36. Name the two male leads in *Red Badge of Courage*.
37. Rick's last name in *Casablanca*?
38. First names of the Andrew Sisters.
39. Who was the "Brazilian Bombshell"?
40. Who was the Sweater Girl?
41. Who was the "Oomph Girl"?
42. Who was the "It Girl"?
43. Who was the Bronx Bull?
44. Who was the Bounty Hunter in "Wanted, Dead or Alive"?
45. Who killed Gregory Peck in *The Gunfighter*?
46. Who played the monster in *Abbott and Costello Meet Frankenstein*?
47. Who starred in *Man in the Attic*?
48. What was the name of "The Boston Strangler"?
49. What time can we expect Frank Miller?
50. Name Charlie Chan's chauffeur and friend.

And remember, funseekers. Whatever else you do today, you find somebody to be nice to.